FINANCE FOR SHOPPING CENTER NONFINANCIAL PROFESSIONALS

FINANCE FOR SHOPPING CENTER NONFINANCIAL PROFESSIONALS

International Council of Shopping Centers
New York

ABOUT THE INTERNATIONAL COUNCIL OF SHOPPING CENTERS

The International Council of Shopping Centers (ICSC) is the trade association of the shopping center industry. Serving the shopping center industry since 1957, ICSC is a not-for-profit organization with over 40,000 members in 77 countries worldwide.

ICSC members include shopping center
- owners
- developers
- managers
- marketing specialists
- leasing agents
- retailers
- researchers
- attorneys
- architects
- contractors
- consultants
- investors
- lenders and brokers
- academics
- public officials

ICSC sponsors more than 300 meetings a year and provides a wide array of services and products for shopping center professionals, including publications and research data.

For more information about ICSC, write or call the
International Council of Shopping Centers
1221 Avenue of the Americas
New York, NY 10020-1099
Telephone: 646-728-3800
Fax: 212-589-5555
www.icsc.org

This publication is designed to provide accurate and authoritative information in regard to the subject matter covered. It is sold with the understanding that the publisher is not engaged in rendering legal, accounting, or other professional services. If legal advice or other expert assistance is required, the services of a competent professional person should be sought.

> *—From a Declaration of Principles jointly adopted by a Committee of the American Bar Assocaiton and a Committee of Publishers.*

Published by
International Council of Shopping Centers
Publications Department
1221 Avenue of the Americas
New York, NY 10020-1099

Cover Design: Demark Keller & Gardner Inc.
Text Design: Stanley S. Drate/Folio Graphics Co. Inc.
ICSC Catalog Number: 170
International Standard Book Number: 1-58268-006-X
Printed in the United States of America

Contents

3. The Lease 39
John L. Gerdes, SCSM

4. The Business Plan 63
Kate M. Sheehy

About This Book

As a shopping center professional, you have unique information needs about finance. For example, you need to know how rents are calculated, what information a retailer's sales report provides, and the role the Consumer Price Index serves in the industry, among other areas.

Finance for Shopping Center Nonfinancial Professionals provides you with practical information on financial terms and principles used in the shopping center industry. Each chapter has been contributed by a shopping center professional with financial management expertise. The contributors have clarified explanations of financial terms and principles with examples and formulas specific to shopping centers.

Subjects covered in *Finance for Shopping Center Nonfinancial Professionals* include the following:

- Accounting fundamentals
- The financial statement
- The lease
- The business plan
- Retail leasing
- Rates of return
- Numbers needed to manage your business.

A handy glossary and index is included at the back of this book to help you easily find information.

Acknowledgments

The International Council of Shopping Centers gratefully acknowledges the following shopping center professionals who contributed the chapters that appear in this book:

John L. Bell, CLS
Senior Vice President
Hiffman Shaffer Associates, Inc.
Chicago, Illinois

John L. Gerdes, SCSM
Director of Retail Properties
L&B Realty Advisors, Inc.
Dallas, Texas

Brad M. Hutensky
President
The Hutensky Group
Hartford, Connecticut

Kenneth S. Lamy
President
The Lamy Group, Ltd.
New Orleans, Louisiana

John E. Phelan, CLS
Executive Vice President
New England Development
Newton, Massachusetts

Kate M. Sheehy
Vice President
Jones Lang LaSalle
Atlanta, Georgia

The International Council of Shopping Centers gratefully acknowledges the following individuals and their companies for the time and expertise they offered in reviewing this publication:

John Behling
Vice President, Asset
  Management
General Growth Properties, Inc.
Chicago, Illinois

David P. Carson, CPA
Director, Lease Accounting
Simon Property Group
Indianapolis, Indiana

Carl R. Esser, CSM
Senior Vice President
Clarion Reality Services
Dallas, Texas

Jack R. Greenberg, CPA
Vice President and Director
  Internal Audit and
  Management Services
The Rouse Company
Columbia, Maryland

Mary Kate Herron
Vice President, Retail Sales and
  Tenant Relations
WellsPark Group
Newton, Massachusetts

Brad M. Hutensky
President
The Hutensky Group
Hartfort, Connecticut

Stan Lashner
Managing Director
Lashner, Rush & Associates, Inc.
Horsham, Pennsylvania

FINANCE FOR SHOPPING CENTER NONFINANCIAL PROFESSIONALS

An Introduction to Accounting

Kate M. Sheehy

$\mathbf{M}$any years ago, a bright young individual joined a corporate property management staff just as the annual budget review ritual began. She had worked in multifamily residential real estate and was a whiz with software. The staff members considered themselves especially fortunate to get someone with any related real estate experience.

This newcomer spent her first week on the job attending meetings at which general managers presented their plans. Like many smart people, she did much more listening than speaking, and she took a lot of notes. The following Monday, the young person approached one of the executives to ask a question: she wanted to know what GLA is.

This incident points up an important lesson: Make sure everyone on the team understands and can use the terms being discussed. Imagine how much that new employee missed in nine different budget reviews because no one had explained the term *gross leasable area!* Her experience must have been like watching a foreign-language film with no subtitles.

For many shopping center professionals, accounting and finance terms may as well be spoken in a foreign language. Despite experience in managing or leasing or marketing a shopping center, even veterans are not always as fluent in the language of finance as they would like to be—or as they should be. The need to "talk the talk" is also greater today than in the past. A large number of U.S. shopping centers now are owned by Real Estate Investment Trusts (REITs), which are publicly traded entities. That has focused Wall Street's eye on this business, making shopping centers more of a numbers game than ever before.

The first part of this chapter will cover some accounting concepts, terms, and equations. Then a few finance terms and appraisal concepts will be discussed.

Accounting Basics

Accounting is certainly about numbers—although it may be more fun to think of accounting as being about money. Some people shy away from accounting and finance because they believe that numbers are the same as mathematics. Perhaps they have unpleasant math memories from their school days. Understanding accounting, however, does not begin with numbers; it starts with a system of logic and its language.

In order to keep track of what a company owns and owes, and how much money it earns and spends, someone creates a *chart of accounts,* which is simply an organized list of the company's financial activity codes, the "financial DNA." Each *account* in the chart tracks *transactions,* noting the accumulating financial additions and subtractions. A transaction is expressed in terms of money and generally involves some transfer of value. Think of it as an economic event for the company, with the most basic transactions being sales and purchases. There are five main categories of accounts: *assets, liabilities, equity, revenues,* and *expenses.*

Assets are what a company owns, and *liabilities* are what a company owes. *Equity* is the owner's interest in the company after all obligations are met. If the subject were your personal finances, your home would be an asset and your mortgage a liability. The difference between the value of your home and the balance of your mortgage is your equity.

Revenues are what the company receives for its products or services. Your revenue is your salary; a shopping center's revenues are its rents and other charges. *Expenses* are what a company pays out to make a product or deliver a service. Your expenses include a utility bill for your home. Likewise, a shopping center has utility expenses—just a little greater than yours.

An accountant or bookkeeper keeps the collection of all these accounts in a *ledger,* often called the *general ledger.* In the days before computers, ledgers were books with a separate page for every account. Other books, called *journals,* were used to record the original entry and the details for the various accounts. You may have heard this process of recording called *journal entry.* To illustrate, the accounts receivable journal tells you which tenant currently owes how much. When those amounts are added up, your accountant records the total in the general ledger, in an account called *accounts receivable.* The process of transferring information from the journal to the ledger is called *posting.*

The foundation of accounting is something called *double-entry book-keeping.* (This does not imply keeping two sets of books containing different information.) Double-entry bookkeeping means that for every addition, there must be a subtraction, so that the totals remain balanced. To be comfortable with this concept, many people find it best to visualize a T to describe any account. On the bar of the T is the name of the account. On the left side of the T's downstroke are listed all *debits;* on the right, *credits.* The left side is used to record increases in some accounts; the right side, increases in others. The left side accumulates pluses—positive signs; the right side accumulates minuses—negative signs.

When posting to the ledger, there must be a credit for every debit. Debits must equal credits, and vice versa. Bear in mind that the way to increase an asset account (what a company owns) is opposite to the way you increase a liability account (what a company owes). Imagine, for example, that you decide to buy a boat, but you do not put any money down on it; you borrow the full amount of the purchase price. Now you own that boat, and it is one of your assets. Yet you owe the mortgage company, so that obligation is one of your liabilities.

Here is how different accounts work:

- An increase to an asset account is a debit.
- An increase to a liability account is a credit.
- An increase to an equity account is a credit.
- An increase to a revenue account is a credit.
- An increase to an expense account is a debit.

You may never have a need to use T accounts, but if your accounting colleagues start drawing Ts, now you know that they are figuring out how they will record a certain transaction on the ledger. For instance, if you want to record the boat purchase mentioned above, you need a couple of accounts. First, set up an asset account, and remember that additions to assets are debits, which are recorded on the left side of the T. If the boat cost $30,000, write $30,000 on the left side of the T for your asset account. Second, you have a loan, which is a liability. Increases to liabilities are credits, which are recorded on the right side of the T. On your liability T, write $30,000 on the right side.

Boat		Loan	
Debit	Credit	Debit	Credit
$30,000			$30,000

Notice that if you add the debits (pluses) and the credits (minuses) together, they zero out. No transaction is fully recorded until the debits equal the credits.

Financial Statements

Although the ledger is a place for account information to reside, it is not an effective communication tool. Ownership and management need to understand the results of operations and the financial condition of a firm. Think of it as a scorecard.

The accounting scorecard is a set of *financial statements.* The two primary statements are a *balance sheet,* which shows the financial condition of the company at a point in time, and an *operating statement.* The operating statement is probably more familiar to shopping center managers. Also known as a *profit-and-loss statement (P&L)* or an *income statement,* the operating statement measures the results of operations. It shows revenues and expenses by specific categories and reports profit or loss for the current *accounting period.* An accounting period could be a month, a quarter, or a year. A twelve-month accounting period is called a *fiscal year.* If the accounting period ends on December 31, then the company uses a calendar year for its fiscal year.

There are two other financial statements that are very important to your accountants and auditors but not as likely to be used by the nonfinancial professional. The first is a *statement of cash flow,* which measures the change in cash position during the period. The second is the *statement of retained earnings,* which reconciles the balance of the retained earnings from the beginning to the end of the year. Retained earnings will be discussed further later in this chapter.

When a U.S. company is publicly owned and traded on a stock exchange, the company is required to file its financial statements with the Securities and Exchange Commission (SEC) for public disclosure. The *10K* is the annual such filing or financial statement with all supporting schedules. The *10Q* is a quarterly financial statement, also required.

An annual report includes management's discussion of performance for the year and the financial statements, for details. The annual report is generally prepared for an external audience, including stockholders, analysts, lenders, and other parties interested in the company's performance.

OPERATING STATEMENT

Various formulas describe the composition of a financial statement. For the operating statement, this is the formula:

$$\text{Revenues} - \text{Expense} = \text{Income}$$

In the statement, revenues are listed first and totaled. Expenses are listed second and totaled. The difference between the two is income.

There are refinements to the way income is described in an operating statement. In the formula above, there are no distinctions regarding the types of revenue or types of expense. Sometimes, however, an owner or manager wants more detail. In particular, the executive wants to know the profitability of the firm's operations. *Net operating income* (NOI) is calculated by subtracting the *operating expenses* from the revenue. Operating expenses are all expenses, occuring periodically, used to produce the sales or revenue of the firm, except for *depreciation.*

Before examining depreciation in the next section, note some differences between *net income* and net operating income as applied to shopping centers. This is done by looking at the components, that is, either revenues or expenses. To understand the distinctions between net income and NOI, start by recognizing the company's primary source of revenue. For a shopping center, this is the rent received from tenants, based upon their lease terms.

Now, say the owner of a shopping center has excess cash on hand for part of the year, kept in an interest-bearing account. Some would argue that the interest revenue is not part of operating income, because it is not directly generated by the operation of the center. Similarly, they would exclude revenue received for selling (at a gain) equipment such as a vehicle, because selling equipment is not a direct part of the operation of a center or its primary business.

Another such example is the money a tenant pays for an early lease termination. That revenue will not recur; in other words, it will not be there next year and the year after that, but is instead a one-time event. Therefore, many firms exclude such payments from NOI. Other companies include only the portion of the payment equal to the amount of rent the tenant would have paid had it stayed through the date when a replacement tenant starts paying. This treatment reflects the intent of the termination agreement to compensate the landlord for lost rent.

Certain expenses may be excluded for similar reasons. Perhaps some attorney's or consultant's fees would be excluded because they were not expenses of the current day-to-day ongoing operation.

Recall the idea that financial statements are the scorecard of a company. NOI is one way to keep score. But each company can define its own NOI, deciding what counts in the score and what does not. Strictly speaking, NOI is not a pure accounting term. If you reviewed a company's 10K or the audited financial statements, you might not find a line in the operating statement labeled NOI. Rather, you are more likely to find NOI as a line item in the monthly operating statements prepared for internal purposes. So if you want to know how to calculate your company's NOI, the best way is to ask the accountants in your company how they calculate it.

Two other measurements are similar to NOI: *Earnings Before Interest, Taxes, Depreciation, and Amortization (EBITDA)* and *Funds From Operations (FFO)*. EBITDA is used in financial-statement supplemental disclosures by public companies. It began as a benchmark employed by analysts for companies other than real estate firms. When ownership of many U.S. shopping centers came to be held by REITs, Wall Street analysts began to apply the measurement to real estate firms as well. EBITDA attempts to measure a company's operations by eliminating charges such as depreciation and focusing on the results from operations without either interest revenue or expense. EBITDA approximates the total cash from operations.

You might be wondering what the difference is between EBITDA and *cash flow*. Cash flow is the spendable income available after all payments are made, including mortgage principal and interest. Cash flow recognizes the timing of receipts and payments. If a tenant owes rent for March but does not pay it until May, cash flow will add the receipt in May. EBITDA, on the other hand, will recognize the receipt in March, when the lease says the payment is due.

FFO is a bottom-line measurement favored by REITs. This is a benchmark that analysts use. FFO approximates the cash-generating power of a company. Unlike EBITDA, FFO does not concentrate strictly on what is produced from the primary operations of the firm but instead looks at total cash.

NOI, EBITDA, and FFO are the *bottom line;* each measures profitability of the operations of a shopping center or portfolio of properties. Determining which one will be used is a function of both the ownership structure and the management firm for your shopping center. The bottom line is the score; the answer to how your company's score is kept can best be found in your accounting department. Ask whether your company uses NOI, EBITDA, or FFO, so you know how your property is performing relative to the company's measurement.

Depreciation and Amortization. Some expenses and, as the examples above describe, some revenues are recorded in the operating statement after NOI, or "below the line." (The "line" is the bottom line.) Such expenses include *depreciation* and *amortization*. Depreciation applies to *tangible assets;* amortization, to *intangible assets.* Tangible assets are physical assets such as buildings, vehicles, and equipment. Intangible assets are generally characterized by a lack of physical existence. Tenant allowances, for example, can be considered intangible. While a tenant may have used an allowance to build out a store, you cannot specifically identify the physical form of the allowance. You cannot attach an inventory tag to the allowance.

Both depreciation and amortization are frequently referred to as *noncash charges,* because the amounts recorded in those accounts do not represent expenditures in the current accounting period. Instead, the amounts represent the economic value received in the current year from an asset.

What does that mean? Go back to your $30,000 boat. When you purchased the boat, you made a *capital expenditure.* A capital expenditure is a purchase of something you expect to last for at least a year—one or more accounting periods. When you make a capital expenditure, you acquire an asset.

Say you expected the boat to have a *useful life* of ten years. An asset's useful life is the period of time you expect to get value for your purchase. Maybe you keep it longer, maybe not. At the time of the purchase, however, you thought it would last ten years before it wore out or became obsolete.

If you used a method of depreciation called *straight-line depreciation,* in which an expense is recognized in equal amounts over the useful life of the asset, you would record expense of $3,000 each year for ten years. Now is a good time to let T accounts describe what will happen.

There are two accounts in the ledger for depreciation. One is an expense account. The other is a balance-sheet account called a *contra-asset account,* because it works opposite to the way an asset account works. Additions to a contra-asset account are recorded on the right side of the T; they are credits.

Year 1:

Boat

Debit	Credit
$30,000	

Depreciation: Boat		**Depreciation Expense**	
Debit	Credit	Debit	Credit
	$3,000	$3,000	

Year 2:

Depreciation: Boat		**Depreciation Expense**	
Debit	Credit	Debit	Credit
	$6,000	$3,000	

Year 3:

Depreciation: Boat		**Depreciation Expense**	
Debit	Credit	Debit	Credit
	$9,000	$3,000	

You already have an asset account called "Boat" with $30,000 on the left side (debit). In year one, you record $3,000 in your contra-asset account—named depreciation—and enter it on the right side of the **T** (credit). The corresponding $3,000 entry is in your expense account on the left side of the **T** (debit). At the end of three years, as illustrated above, the total of the contra-asset account will be a credit of $9,000. At the end of ten years, the total depreciation is $30,000, completely offsetting the $30,000 asset. In other words, after ten years, the asset has a value of zero.

Year 10:

Boat		**Depreciation: Boat**	
Debit	**Credit**	**Debit**	**Credit**
$30,000			$30,000

Remember that amortization applies to intangible assets; these assets are not physical in nature. Probably the most common examples for a shopping center are tenant allowances and lease commissions. Making an expenditure for either of those does not add something on which you can put an inventory tag. Both are assets, however, because these capital expenditures help make a lease happen and a store open, generating rent for the center. In these cases, the useful life is the term of the lease.

If a landlord paid a $60,000 allowance to a tenant with a seven-year lease term and paid the management company $10,000 in commission, what would the first year's amortization be? Using the straight-line method, it would be $10,000 or ($60,000 + $10,000) divided by seven years. Please note that the ledger would have one account for amortization of the allowance and another for the commission.

There are other methods of depreciation beside straight-line. They work in generally the same way, but they may accelerate the process or get to zero faster. Frequently these alternative methods are used for tax purposes to allow a firm to recognize more expense in order to reduce the amount of income subject to tax. Once again, it is best to ask how your company calculates depreciation.

BALANCE SHEET

As with the operating statement, there is a formula for the balance sheet:

$$\text{Assets} = \text{Liabilities} + \text{Equity, or}$$
$$\text{Equity} = \text{Assets} - \text{Liabilities}$$

Walk through the creation of a balance sheet by imagining the beginning of a shopping center. First, there is an ownership entity. Say it's an equal partnership of Mr. Johnson and Ms. Brown. Each of them invests $5,000,000 in the new firm and places the money in a bank account. To record this event, there is an asset called Cash in Bank, with a balance of $10,000,000. The firm has no liabilities, so where does the corresponding entry go? Using the formula above, there is now an equity of $10,000,000.

Next, the partnership purchases land for $1,000,000. This decreases the Cash in Bank account and adds an asset called Land. Now they construct a building for $3,200,000, again decreasing cash and creating an asset. To fill the center, they spend $2,000,000 in tenant allowances and $160,000 in leasing commissions. Cash is reduced again and assets are recorded. Then they take out a mortgage for $4,000,000. This creates a liability of $4,000,000 but adds cash back in the same amount. What is their equity? Here is the balance sheet:

Johnson and Brown
Balance Sheet

Assets

Cash in Bank	$ 7,640,000
Land	1,000,000
Building	3,200,000
Tenant Allowances	2,000,000
Leasing Commissions	160,000
Total Assets	$14,000,000

Liabilities

Mortgage	$ 4,000,000
Total Liabilities	$ 4,000,000

Equity

Mr. Johnson	$ 5,000,000
Ms. Brown	5,000,000
Total Equity	$10,000,000
Total Liabilities and Equity	$14,000,000

If you have any trouble figuring out how this balance sheet ended up this way, it may be because there is no step-by-step record here showing each addition and subtraction. In real cases, your accountants would leave an *audit trail* to explain what happened. An audit trail is an explicit set of documentation (either paper copies or information traced by an accounting software program) that illustrates how each entry made its way into the books.

Remember that the financial statements are a presentation of the account information stored in the general ledger. Look at the activity in the Johnson and Brown cash account:

	Cash	
	Debit	**Credit**
(initial investment)	10,000,000	
		1,000,000 (land)
		3,200,000 (building)
		2,000,000 (tenant allowance)
		160,000 (lease commissions)
(mortgage proceeds)	4,000,000	
	14,000,000	6,360,000

The difference between the debits and credits in the cash account is a debit of $7,640,000, which matches the account as shown on the balance sheet. The balance sheet and the operating statement are only presentations of the account information in the general ledger.

If you were to similarly track each balance-sheet line item, you would illustrate another fundamental: assets have to come from somewhere. Either equity was contributed or other assets were reduced or liabilities were taken to create the assets of the Johnson-Brown partnership

Appraisal Concepts

Understanding *value* is critical for any real estate professional. This section is only introductory. *Appraisal* concepts—related to how the value of a property is determined—are presented in detail in chapter 6, "Understanding Rates of Return."

If the financial statements are like the scorecard of a game, then you could consider the appraisal to be the overall statistics for the season. The appraisal tells the larger story, the big picture.

Remember that the balance sheet shows the financial condition of the firm on a particular date. The activity in the asset, liabilities, and equity accounts accumulates over time. Equity is what is left over after obligations of the firm are met; it is the owner's interest in the business.

Equity, however, is not the same as value. The value of a business, in this case a shopping center, arises from the income it produces year after year—its operating income. To calculate value, you capitalize that stream of income, essentially by applying a percentage rate to the income stream. This percentage rate is called a *cap (capitalization) rate.*

The most important thing to remember about value is that it is set in the marketplace. What you have to sell is worth only what someone else will pay. Is your Beanie Baby worth $1,000? Only if you can find a collector willing to give you $1,000 for it.

Likewise, cap rates are a function of the market. When someone buys a shopping center, the purchaser is making an investment and also giving up the opportunity to invest in other things. One way to think about cap rates is to consider them to be the rate of return a buyer is willing to receive for an investment. Cap rates can be affected by unlimited factors such as perceived risk, creditworthiness, competition, and a property's upside potential. With cap rates, like golf scores, lower is better—at least for the seller. The lower the cap rate, the better the market value of the center.

Typically, to calculate value for a shopping center, an appraiser will apply a cap rate to income for multiple years. There are occasions in which a buyer and seller negotiate a price based on only one year's income. To illustrate, assume that a center produces net operating income of $1,000,000 and the cap rate is 10 percent (stated as a decimal, 0.10). Here is the value calculation:

$$\frac{\text{Income}}{\text{Rate}} = \text{Value, or } \frac{\$1,000,000}{0.10} = \$10,000,00$$

You might remember this equation as "IRV." The handy thing about the equation is that you can twist it around. Say you knew the shopping center had net operating income of $1,000,000 and that it just sold for $10,000,000. What is the cap rate?

$$\frac{\text{Income}}{\text{Value}} = \text{Rate, or } \frac{\$1,000,000}{\$10,000,000} = 0.10 \text{ (or 10 percent)}$$

Similarly, you can figure out the income if you know the value and the cap rate:

$$\text{Value} \times \text{Rate} = \text{Income, or } \$10,000,000 \times 0.10 = \$1,000,000$$

As noted previously, the lower a cap rate, the better for the seller. Take a look at the same center with $1 million net operating income. If you used a 9 percent cap rate, what is the value?

$$\frac{\text{Income}}{\text{Rate}} = \text{Value, or } \frac{\$1,000,000}{.09} = \$11,111,111$$

Notice that a 1 percent change in the cap rate created an additional $1,111,111 in value. Why would a buyer pay more for one shopping center than another? Or why would a buyer accept a lower rate of return? As noted earlier, there are almost unlimited factors in that decision. However, one is the quality of the income stream.

MARKET RENT

Rent for shopping center space is subject to the same market rules as Beanie Babies: it is the rent that a willing tenant will pay. More technically, *market rent* is the rate at which space would be leased if offered in a competitive market.

For example, assume that a variety store in a center court location is paying $5 per square foot because the tenant executed a thirty-year lease with options in 1979. By 1999, other tenants in the center court are paying $35 per square foot. What is the market rent for a vacant space in the center court? It is probably much closer to $35 than to $5, because there are tenants willing to pay $35 in today's market, given the success of the center and the location of the space.

Determining market rent is essential to the appraisal process. Because an appraisal typically considers an income stream over several years, an appraiser must make assumptions about the rates at which vacant space will lease and at which tenants will renew in future years. The appraiser must consider at least two factors about the center: the sales it produces and its dominance in the trade area. The first factor is important because tenants determine their willingness to pay by the sales they expect to achieve; the second, because the caliber of tenants the center will attract depends on shopper preferences and loyalty. The better the merchandise array meets the shopper's demands and desires, the stronger the sales performance of the center will be.

In an appraisal, all vacancies may be given the same market rent as part of the assumptions. In reality, however, different spaces will command different rents based on their size, proximity to center court or to anchor stores, and quality. Sight lines or configuration may affect quality. Different market rents might even apply to the same space if tenants of different merchandise categories are considered.

The term *market rent* is sometimes used interchangeably with *budgeted rent* or even *appraisal rent.* Budgeted rent is only the target approved by ownership for the annual plan. Most owners reserve the right to approve the terms for individual leases as they are submitted. Even appraisal rent is only as good a number as the assumptions used at a point in time. Is the center court space still worth $35 per square foot if the construction of a new center, anchored by a major upscale department store, is announced for a site just up the highway?

OTHER FACTORS

Besides the quality of the income stream, there are other considerations in determining quality and formulating the appraisal assumptions. One of these is *rate of retention;* another is *credit loss.* These terms are introduced here, but you will find a detailed discussion of these and other considerations in chapter 6, "Understanding the Rate of Return."

The rate of retention is the rate at which existing tenants renew their leases in their existing spaces. As noted earlier, the appraiser must establish rents for renewing tenants. The first step is to determine how many tenants, and which ones, will renew. Sometimes an appraiser will rely on historical data to decide what likelihood exists that a tenant or group of tenants will renew.

If, for example, two-thirds of the expiring tenant leases were renewed over the last three to five years, the appraiser may use a rate of retention of 66 percent. This translates into 34 percent of the expiring space becoming available to rent to new tenants. Identifying nonrenewals may be a particularly important part of the process if current market rents are much higher than average rents for existing leases. Tenants who renew in place may be unwilling to pay market rents if the increase over their current rate is too high. In a successful center, however, new tenants might be willing to pay more.

Since value derives from income, consider one example of the impact of a new tenant versus a renewing tenant. Say Tenant A is paying $22 per square foot in minimum rent. Even with *overage rent,* a percentage of the tenant's total annual sales paid in addition to minimum rent, Tenant A pays only $27 per square foot in effective rent. Upon renewal, Tenant A may be willing to pay $30 per square foot in base rent—a 10 percent increase over the current total rent. Tenant B, however, may be willing to pay $35 per square foot.

If Tenant A is valuable to the merchandise mix and is producing good sales levels, a landlord might decide to renew the lease and find another location for Tenant B. If, however, Tenant A does not present an attractive storefront or does not offer the most appropriate merchandise for the trade area, the landlord might decide not to renew the lease. The landlord determines that Tenant B represents a better merchandising decision as well as willingness to pay a higher rent. This does not preclude offering Tenant A another location, but that would probably be subject to a different market rent.

Credit loss is the expected percentage of revenue that will be lost from one or more tenants due to nonpayment, or noncollection, of rent. In an appraisal, the rents from all tenants in the center will be accumulated to calculate income and value. In reality, not all rents will be collected.

If rent is not collected, if there is no cash being generated, there is no value created. Therefore, the appraiser will determine some percentage of revenue to deduct before calculating value. Like the rate of retention, this credit loss percentage may also be based on historical averages. The appraiser may even elect to use more than one rate, applying a lower risk to credit tenants than to local, "mom and pop" operators. *Credit tenants* are generally national chains with strong financial statements.

For purposes of determining revenue, most appraisers will consider the center leased at up to 100 percent occupancy to create *gross potential revenue. Vacancy loss* recognizes that a property will not always be 100 percent leased. To calculate vacancy loss, a percentage is applied to the gross revenue, and the resulting amount is deducted. If the appraiser believes that the center will stabilize at 95 percent occupancy, a 5 percent vacancy loss rate will be applied to gross revenue. At the very least, the vacancy loss rate anticipates that not all tenants will live out the terms of their leases. For one reason or another, some tenants will terminate early. This leaves a vacancy in the center for at least as long as it takes to find a replacement tenant.

Perhaps you are a general manager whose annual incentive is based on meeting certain NOI (net operating income) targets. If financial statements can be considered a way to keep score, then understanding the scorekeeping rules seems like a good idea when so much is at stake. This section will discuss two different accounting bases, general rules, and the accounting cycle, as well as a couple of rules that are commonly misunderstood.

Cash versus Accrual Accounting

The *cash basis method of accounting* is a system whereby revenues and expenses are recognized when cash is received or paid. Your personal accounting for income tax uses the cash basis. For income, you report only the money you actually received. If you were entitled to a bonus for 1998 but were not paid until 1999, you recognized the revenue in 1999. Similarly, if you owed real estate taxes for the calendar year 1998 but your local jurisdiction did not bill you until 1999, you reported that expense when you paid it in 1999.

Even when a firm does not use cash basis accounting, the company may need to prepare cash-flow statements. This is not the same as keeping books on the cash basis but still requires that cash inflows and outflows be tracked. This obligation is relatively common for shopping centers whose ownership is required to make quarterly dividend payments. A similar requirement may exist when a property's mortgage is underwritten based upon expectations of cash flow, and the terms of the loan require cash-flow statements.

Public companies must maintain their records on the *accrual basis method of accounting.* This system recognizes revenue when earned and expense as incurred, regardless of whether cash is received or paid out. For instance, in a shopping center, rents are recognized as revenue on the first of the month when the tenant leases state that rents are due. Even if rents are uncollected by the end of the same month, the revenue is recorded.

Expense is similarly entered in the period during which either the goods or services are received. If a third party provides the shopping center's security, for instance, you would record the expense for that month's public safety service even if you did not receive the vendor's invoice until the following month. An *accrual* is the entry made to record a bill not yet received (or an income item not yet collected).

Many people have trouble knowing what to provide for accruals. Usually, it just means listing all the things you have not paid for yet. If you process payments to vendors from your shopping center, then you know what you have paid. Say you received a shipment of light bulbs in the month of December but did not write a check for it until January; then you would accrue the expense for the light bulbs in December.

Suppose, however, that your company writes checks from a central location, and all checks for the month are processed by the twentieth day. You receive the shipment of light bulbs on December 20. Even if you submit a bill for payment the very day you receive the light bulbs, the vendor will not be paid until January because all checks for the month are already processed. You have to accrue the expense for the light bulbs in December. The point is that you need to understand your company's check-processing schedule in order to submit accurate accruals.

Another thing that confounds people is the reversal of accruals. Since an accrual is not a payment and may even be an estimate of expense, it must be reversed in the following month. Then, when the actual expense is recorded, there will be one item recognized, not two.

For example, go back to the public safety expense. When asked for an accrual, the general manager submitted $50,000 as the amount for January. The accountant recorded a debit of $50,000. In February, the accountant reversed the accrual by recording a credit for $50,000. Sometime during February, the January bill was paid in the amount of $51,800. At the end of February, the general manager accrued another $50,000.

Security Expense

	Debit	Credit
(January accrual)	50,000	
		50,000 (January accrual reversed)
(January payment processed)	51,800	
(February accrual)	50,000	

When the February books were closed, the security account totaled $101,800—two months of expense. Thus, expense was matched to the period in which the public safety company provided the service.

Generally Accepted Accounting Principles (GAAP)

Generally accepted accounting principles, or *GAAP* (pronounced "gap"), constitute an authoritative set of rules adopted by the accounting profession. These rules dictate the way a business reports its financial condition and performance. For instance, GAAP requires accrual basis accounting. GAAP rules apply to many industries, but one rule has a particular impact on real estate.

Straight-line rents are the amounts recorded to amortize rents evenly over the term of the lease. As an example, consider a seven-year lease with three months of free rent and a step increase at the beginning of the fourth year. For simplicity's sake, this tenant opens on January 1 in 2,500 square feet, paying an initial rent of $15 per square foot, increasing to $18 in the fourth year.

Table 1.1 The Straight-Lining Process

	Lease Rent	Entry	Straight-Line Rent
Year 1	$ 28,125	$12,321	$ 40,446
Year 2	37,500	2,947	40,447
Year 3	37,500	2,946	40,446
Year 4	45,000	(4,554)	40,446
Year 5	45,000	(4,553)	40,447
Year 6	45,000	(4,554)	40,446
Year 7	45,000	(4,553)	40,447
	$283,125	0	$283,125

Notice that the straight-line entry is negative in the later years of the lease. What benefits revenue in the early years turns unfavorable toward the end of the lease-term. Some companies record these amounts in a separate account listed below net operating income on the operating statement. Others, however, list the account with all other rent accounts. This is worth mentioning if you have struggled to figure out a variance in rent between two years, only to find that you forgot straight-lining.

Bad Debt and the Allowance for Doubtful Accounts

Now is a good time to mention another source of confusion: bad debt. In the accrual method of accounting, an estimate of the amounts that may not be collected from tenants is recorded in an expense account labeled Bad Debt. As noted previously, the expense entry will be a debit. The corresponding credit is recorded in a contra-asset account labeled Allowance for Doubtful Accounts. This entry accomplishes two things: first, it reduces current period income for the anticipated noncollection of rent; second, using the contra-asset account, it reduces accounts receivable on the balance sheet so as not to overstate assets.

For our example, say a brand-new center bills $350,000 per month in rent and charges. The manager estimates that the uncollected portion of rent will be 5 percent. These are the first month's entries, illustrated with T accounts:

Rent		Accounts Receivable	
Debit	**Credit**	**Debit**	**Credit**
	$350,000	$350,000	

Bad Debt Expense		Allowance for Doubtful Accts.	
Debit	**Credit**	**Debit**	**Credit**
$17,500			$17,500

Keeping straight with bad debt is a little easier if you recall that the additions you make to the current-period expense account have corresponding additions to the allowance account. The object is to make additions (or subtractions) sufficient to keep the balance of the allowance adequate to cover uncollectible accounts receivable. Companies have different policies for determining the adequacy of the allowance. Most use the aged accounts receivable report as a guide. A common practice is to ensure that the allowance is at least equal to all accounts outstanding for 120 days or more.

The Accounting Cycle

This chapter previously covered the first three steps of the accounting cycle:

- Individual transactions
- Recording in a journal
- Posting the transaction summaries to the general ledger.

The next step is to prepare a *trial balance.* This is a list of all open accounts in the ledger with their balances. When the trial balance is complete, debits and credits will prove equal. The trial balance also provides the list necessary to prepare the financial statements.

As an example, consider the earlier story of Mr. Johnson and Ms. Brown and the center they built. The partners lease this 40,000-square-foot specialty center to 100 percent occupancy on October 1—Grand Opening Day for Enterprise Shops. The rents for the center average $20 per square foot. The extra charges in the tenants' leases, such as common-area maintenance and real estate taxes, completely recover the center's expenses. Therefore, all rent is profit to the center. After the partners deduct $100,000 for three months' interest on the mortgage, the operating statement for December 31 shows net income of $100,000.

Here is the trial balance for the end of the year:

Enterprise Shops
Trial Balance
December 31, 1999

Account	Debit	Credit
Cash	$ 7,740,000	
Land	1,000,000	
Building	3,200,000	
Tenant Allowances	2,000,000	
Leasing Commissions	160,000	
Mortgage		$4,000,000
Equity: Mr. Johnson		5,000,000
Equity: Ms. Brown		5,000,000
Rent		200,000
Interest Expense	100,000	
	$14,200,000	$14,200,000

Please note that extra charges and expenses have not been included, in order to keep the example pretty basic. In a real financial statement, once the trial balance was completed, there would be some adjusting entries such as accruals, depreciation, or adjustments to the allowance for doubtful accounts.

Instead, skip right to the next step, which is to prepare financial statements. Start with the income statement for Enterprise Shops as of December 31:

Enterprise Shops
Operating Statement
January 1 through December 31, 1999

Revenue

Rent ($20 × 40,000 s.f. × 3 months)	$200,000
Extra Charges	
Total Revenue	$200,000

Expenses

Net Operating Income	$200,000
Interest	100,000
Net Income	$100,000

A major difference between the balance sheet and the operating statement has to do with time and timing. The balance sheet is often called a snapshot, or a picture of the financial condition of the firm at a particular point in time. Balance sheet accounts—assets, liabilities, and equity—accumulate transactions over the life of the firm. An operating statement, on the other hand, is used to present the results of a full or partial accounting period. At the end of the accounting period, operating-statement accounts—revenues and expenses—are "turned back" to zero. Special journal entries, called *closing entries,* are made to reverse all account balances.

Because net income represents the difference between revenue and expense accounts, an entry must be made to adjust the difference. Unless that difference (profit or loss) is distributed back to ownership, an entry is made to an equity account called *retained earnings.* Retained earnings represent the profit or loss held in the company. The balance sheet after closing entries are made is shown on page 22.

Enterprise Shops
Balance Sheet
December 31, 1999

Assets

Cash in Bank	$ 7,740,000
Land	1,000,000
Building	3,200,000
Tenant Allowances	2,000,000
Leasing Commissions	160,000
Total Assets	$14,100,000

Liabilities

Mortgage	$ 4,000,000
Total Liabilities	$ 4,000,000

Equity

Mr. Johnson	$ 5,000,000
Ms. Brown	5,000,000
Retained Earnings	100,000
Total Equity	$10,100,000
Total Liabilities and Equity	$14,100,000

As noted earlier, assets must come from somewhere. Johnson and Brown's partnership demonstrates that the contribution of equity and the assumption of liabilities create assets. Now, wrapping up the operating statement illustrates that leaving profits in the business also creates assets. If Johnson and Brown distributed the earnings to themselves, there would be no retained earnings and cash—an asset—would be reduced.

One additional step in financial-statement preparation is to have all such statements audited by Certified Public Accountants (CPAs). This step subjects the records of the firm to an independent examination for accuracy, completeness, and compliance to GAAP. During the audit, the CPA firm will test processes to establish that the company has adequate *internal controls.* These are the safeguards put in place to help detect errors and prevent all types of employee dishonesty. The audit allows external audiences to have greater confidence in the financial statements that a company publishes.

To recap the accounting cycle, here are the steps:

1. Recognize individual transactions.
2. Record the transactions in a journal.
3. Post the transaction summaries to the general ledger.

4. Prepare a trial balance.
5. Make adjusting entries.
6. Prepare the financial statement.
7. Make closing entries.
8. Audit the statements.

Kate M. Sheehy is Vice President at Jones Lang LaSalle, Atlanta, Georgia.

2 | The Financial Statement

John Bell, CLS

The Purposes of Financial Statements

Many nonfinancial professionals lack a fundamental understanding of the various components of financial statements and how they can be used. When reviewing any financial report, it is important to understand its objective and to recognize the relevance and limitations of the information being considered. The following are important objectives of financial statements:

- To discern what is happening with the economic resource flows
- To gauge or measure progress
- To determine performance over a given period of time
- To assess where an organization or entity stands financially at a given point in time.

All financial statements are not created equal, due to generally accepted accounting principles (GAAP), which allow flexibility in how certain financial transactions are reported. Given the number of off-the-shelf accounting programs that are available, it is a good idea to review financial statements that have been prepared by a certified public account, CPA.

Financial statements can vary as a result of unique characteristics within different industries. For example, some industries require large investment in fixed assets such as property and equipment, while others may require very little. Pricing structure can vary among industries too, which can impose either high or low profit margins. Some industries, such as apparel retailing, are characterized by lenient credit terms, while others sell for cash only, as in the case of fast-food restaurants. Financial statements can even vary among companies in the same industry due to management policy, management competence, and the use of financial leverage or equity.

When reviewing financial statements, it is important to ensure that they cover at least a full year. Due to the seasonality of the shopping center industry, results can easily be distorted when only a partial year is considered. The more financial history you have, the easier it is to measure financial performance. Many financial statements actually contain annual and monthly financial transaction variances, which allow a quick comparison of past and present performance.

Financial statements should help answer questions such as:

- Will a company be able to meet its obligations to pay suppliers, lenders, landlords, and others?
- How risky are the financial and business commitments?
- How profitable is the company?
- How solvent or liquid is the company?
- How efficiently is the company being operated?

Answering these questions requires a good understanding of the three basic components of the GAAP financial statement, which are:

1. The balance sheet
2. The income statement, or profit-and-loss statement
3. The statement of cash flows.

In addition to these components, financial statements usually contain *footnotes,* which explain how certain accounting transactions—such as fiscal/annual periods, depreciation, cash and cash equivalents,[1] marketable securities, and inventories—are treated. Do

---

[1]Cash equivalents are short-term investments that can easily be converted into cash with minimal delay. Examples include money market funds and Treasury bills. They represent investment of excess cash not needed immediately.

not overlook the footnotes. They are an important source of information when reviewing a financial statement.

As illustrated below, financial statements are summarized reports of accounting transactions. Each component reports on different financial transactions and provides information that can be used to measure, gauge, and assess the financial condition of an operating entity.[2]

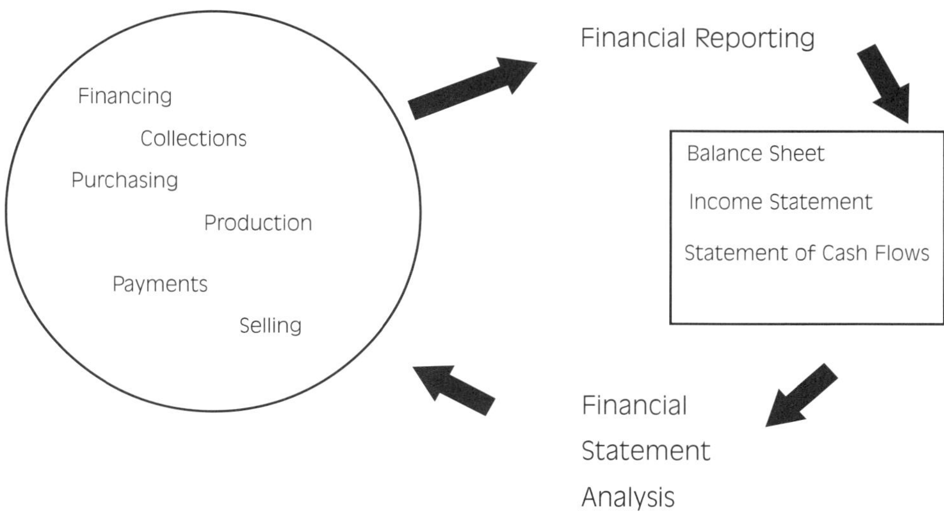

The Basic Structure of a Financial Statement

THE BALANCE SHEET

The balance sheet can best be described as a snapshot of the financial position at a given moment in time. In other words, it depicts the company's assets, liabilities, and equity as of a certain date. It is always a good idea to have the most current report, because receiving income, purchasing assets, and paying expenses will all cause the balance sheet to change over time. The following demonstrates the basic structure of the balance sheet:

$$\text{Assets} = \text{Equities}$$
or,
$$\text{Assets} = \text{Liabilities} + \text{Equities (sometimes called net worth)}$$

---

[2]Operating entity could mean shopping center, corporation, partnership, public company, or organization.

Assets are basically economic resources expected to benefit future activities. Some of these include cash, inventories, accounts receivable, property, and equipment. *Equities* are claims against, or interest in, an entity's assets. *Liabilities* are the economic obligations to non-owners.

The balance sheet is used for calculating key financial ratios such as the current ratio, quick ratio, debt-to-equity ratio, and return-on-equity ratio. These ratios and their significance will be discussed later in this chapter.

THE INCOME STATEMENT

The income statement (also called the profit-and-loss statement or operating statement) can be compared to a motion picture. Instead of a single snapshot at a certain moment, it tracks financial events over a specific period of time. It summarizes activities on a monthly, quarterly, or annual basis. It is the journey, while the balance sheet is the destination. It shows how much income was earned or lost and is used to measure performance by matching accomplishments (revenues, sales) to the efforts (cost of goods sold and other expenses).

The income statement is often compared to a corresponding budget, but it is usually summarized in less detail. It focuses on major categories of expenses, instead of individual line-item expenses. It can serve as a guide to anticipating future performance.

The income statement is usually the first thing lenders, landlords, and investors look at when reviewing financial statements. They want to know if the business is profitable—is it making money? Also, expense categories are often compared to industry averages to determine if these are being kept under control. Comparing the historical performance over several time periods is always a better measure than reviewing only one reporting period. The following demonstrates the basic structure of the income statement:

$$\text{Income} - \text{Expenses} = \text{Net Income}$$

The income statement is an integral part of a financial statement and is used to calculate operating margins, net profit margins, inventory turnover, and many other important financial ratios.

THE STATEMENT OF CASH FLOWS

The *statement of cash flows* coincides with the same reporting period as the income statement, but differs in that it reports only on the cash receipts and cash payments. It reveals the relationship of the net income (bottom line) on the income statement to changes in cash balances. Cash balances can decline despite positive net income, and vice versa.

For example, a company's accounts receivable (cash billed, but not received) on the income statement will be adjusted on the statement of cash flows. In addition, depreciation deductions shown on the income statement are adjusted or added back in, because these are paper deductions for tax purposes and not actual cash expenses.

There are three types of activities that affect cash, which are summarized on the statement of cash flows:

  I. Operating activities
     A. Cash inflows
          1. Collections
          2. Interest and dividends collected
     B. Cash outflows
          1. Cash payments to vendors and suppliers
          2. Cash payments to employees
          3. Interest paid
          4. Taxes paid
          5. Other operating cash payments
          6. Other operating expenses
 II. Investing activities
     A. Cash inflows
          1. Sale of property, plant, and equipment
          2. Sale of securities that are not cash equivalents
          3. Receipt of loan payments
     B. Cash outflows
          1. Purchase of property, plant, and equipment
          2. Purchase of securities that are not cash equivalents
          3. Loans made
III. Financing activities
     A. Cash inflows
          1. Cash borrowed from creditors
          2. Equity securities issued

B. Cash outflows
   1. Repayment of amounts borrowed
   2. Repurchase of equity shares
   3. Payments of dividends

Essentially, most companies present their cash from operations by starting with the net income and making adjustments to arrive at operating receipts, minus disbursements. The following is a summary of adjustments to the statement of cash flows:

Operations	+ Receipts from customers or other sources
	− Payments to suppliers, vendors, employees, etc.
Investing	+ Proceeds from noncurrent assets
	− Investments in new noncurrent assets
Financing	+ Proceeds from new stock issues
	+ Proceeds from borrowing
	− Repurchase of stock
	− Retirement of debt
	− Dividends paid to shareholders
	= Net change in cash

The reporting period for the statement of cash flows always corresponds to the reporting period for the income statement and date of the balance sheet. The following diagram illustrates the linkage connecting the balance sheet, income statement, and statement of cash flows:

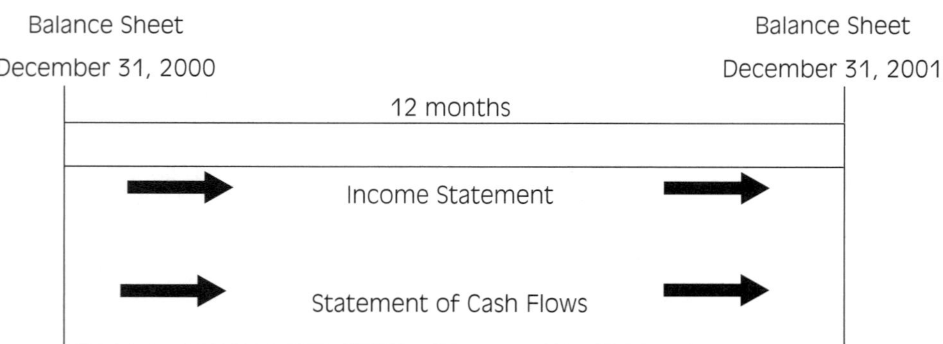

Past cash flows can help predict the need for future cash flows and can aid in determining a company's ability to meet its obligations when due. It provides important information about operating, investing, and financing activities. The statement of cash flows is another important report that is frequently used by analysts, investors, lenders, and landlords.

Constructing a Financial Statement

With a basic understanding of how financial statements are structured, you should now be able to develop the three basic financial statement components. The following is a summary of financial transactions for the XYZ Corporation that occurred during the month of March:

1. Initial investment by owners of $100,000 cash.
2. Acquisition of inventory for $75,000 cash.
3. Acquisition of inventory for $35,000 on open account (accounts payable).
4a. Merchandise sold on open account (accounts receivable) for $120,000.
4b. Merchandise carried in inventory at a cost of $100,000.
5. Cash collections of accounts receivable, $30,000.
6. Cash payments of accounts payable, $10,000.
7a. On March 1, $3,000 disbursed for store rent for the months of March, April, and May.
7b. Rent is $1,000 per month payable quarterly in advance, beginning March 1.

Each of the above transactions can be further organized into a balance-sheet format, as shown in Table 2.1. Then, using the totals from each column in Table 2.1, you can easily develop a balance sheet for the XYZ Corporation, an income statement, and a statement of cash flows. See Tables 2.2, 2.3, and 2.4.

Table 2.1   Summary of XYZ's Financial Transactions for the Month of March

		Assets								Equities			
										Liabilities +		Stockholders' Equity	
	Transactions	Cash	+	Accounts Receivable	+	Inventory	+	Prepaid Rent	=	Accounts Payable	+	Paid-in Capital	+ Retained Income
1.	Initial investment	100,000							=			100,000	
2.	Acquire inventory for cash	(75,000)				75,000			=				
3.	Acquire inventory for credit					35,000			=	35,000			
4a.	Sales on credit			120,000					=				120,000 (revenue)
4b.	Cost of inventory sold					(100,000)			=				(100,000) (expense)
5.	Collect from customers	30,000		(30,000)					=				
6.	Pay accounts of suppliers	(10,000)							=	(10,000)			
7a.	Pay rent in advance	(3,000)						3,000	=				
7b.	Recognize expiration of rental services							(1,000)	=				(1,000) (expense)
	Balance, March 31	42,000	+	90,000	+	10,000	+	2,000	+	25,000	+	100,000	+ 19,000
								$144,000	=	$144,000			

Table 2.2   Balance Sheet for XYZ Corporation as of March 31

Assets		Liabilities	
Cash	$ 42,000	Accounts payable	$ 25,000
Accounts receivable	90,000	Stockholders' equity Paid-in capital	100,000
Inventory	10,000	Retained income	19,000
Prepaid rent	2,000		
TOTALS	$144,000 =		$144,000

Note: The financial transactions balance: Assets = Liabilities + Equities.

Table 2.3   Income Statement for XYZ Corporation as of March 31

Sales (revenues)	$120,000
Expenses	
Cost of goods sold	<$100,000>
Rent	<1,000>
Total expenses	<$101,000>
Net income	$ 19,000

The balance sheet states that there is $42,000 in cash, yet the income statement says there is net income of $19,000. Please note that cash and net income may be related but are not the same. The statement of cash flows makes adjustments to the income statement to arrive at net cash flows:

Table 2.4   Statement of Cash Flows XYZ Corporation as of March 31

Net income	$ 19,000
Adjustments to reconcile cash from the income statement operating activities	
+ Paid-in capital	100,000
− Accounts receivable	<$90,000>
+ Depreciation/amortization	0
− Decrease in inventory	<10,000>
− Prepaid expenses	<2,000>
+ Accounts payable	25,000
Net cash	$42,000

Note: The net cash of $42,000 is the same amount of cash reported on the balance sheet above.

Cash flow, though related to net income, is not equivalent to it. One reason has to do with the accrual method of accounting. Under the accrual method, a transaction is recognized on the income statement when the earnings process is completed. This does not always coincide with the time when cash is being exchanged. For example, goods can be sold on credit (accounts receivable) and accounted for in the income statement although no cash has actually changed hands. Likewise, deductions taken for depreciation are adjusted or added back in because no cash expense has actually occurred.

Ratio Analysis

To help analyze financial statements, investors, analysts, and lenders look at certain ratios, or mathematical relationships, between two or more amounts being reported on. Of primary concern is whether the business will be able to meet its financial obligations when due. Comparing ratios is not the end-all of analysis but can be a good source of benchmarking to the results of similar companies operating in similar circumstances. Ratios are used to measure the following:

- Liquidity
- Solvency
- Profitability
- Operational efficiency.

A very important balance-sheet concept is *working capital,* which is the difference between current assets and current liabilities. Current liabilities are debts due within one year and current assets are those that can be converted to cash in one year or less. Consequently, working capital is the amount of money that is left after all current debts are paid off.

How do you know if there is enough working capital? One way to determine this is to look at the *current ratio.* To find the current ratio, divide the current assets by the current liabilities. A current ratio of 2:1 is generally considered adequate. This means that there is $2 of current assets to support every $1 of current debt.

The *quick ratio* is another important ratio that can be obtained using the balance sheet. Quick assets are what is available to cover a sudden emergency—in other words, readily available cash. To determine quick assets, take the current assets minus inventories, prepaid expenses, and any other illiquid current assets. Then divide the quick-asset figure by the current liabilities. This ratio will tell you what available quick cash there is to cover the current liabilities.

Another important ratio to look at is the *debt-to-equity ratio,* which is an indicator of whether a company is using debt excessively. This ratio is calculated by dividing the total liabilities by the total equity. Some companies can operate using higher debt levels than others. For example, service companies usually operate at higher ratios than manufacturing companies.

The *return-on-equity (ROE) ratio* measures profitability and is often used as "return on investment." This ratio relates the accomplishments (profits) to the resources (investments) provided. The calculation involves dividing annual net income by the average equity.[3] The ROE helps an investor determine if a business is an attractive enterprise in which to invest.

Operating margin helps measure the operational efficiency of a company. For example, the operating margin can be reviewed and compared to similar firms and to the company's own historical performance. Sales[4] may be growing, but operating margins could be declining. The operating margin is determined by dividing the operating income by net sales. This will tell you what percentage of every dollar of sales was retained as profit from operations. The *operating cost ratio* is the complement of the operating margin. For example, if an operating margin were 18.4 percent, the operating cost ratio would be 81.6 percent.

Inventory turnover measures the adequacy and efficiency of the inventory balance. How much inventory should a company have on hand? How many times has it turned historically? How do the inventory turns of a company compare with those of similar companies using the same accounting practices? Once the inventory turnover ratio is calculated, it can be compared to the ratios of similar companies. Note that the proper or average turnover will vary greatly from industry to industry: e.g., fast food, apparel, furniture.

Another ratio used within the shopping center industry is the *occu-*

---

[3]The average equity is calculated by adding the annual reporting period to the previous annual reporting period and dividing that amount by 2.

[4]Total sales before expenses.

pancy cost ratio. This ratio compares a retailer's annual store sales volume to its total annual occupancy costs.[5] For example, a retailer with an annual sales volume of $600,000 and a total annual occupancy cost of 60,000 has an occupancy cost ratio of 10 percent. This ratio is important only when comparing retailers in similar businesses occupying similar properties. The relationship of sales to occupancy costs is used to determine how much base rent a tenant can afford to pay.

The following is a summary of key financial ratios used in analyzing financial statements:

$$\text{Current ratio} = \frac{\text{Current assets}}{\text{Current liabilities}}$$

$$\text{Quick ratio} = \frac{\text{Current assets} - \text{Illiquid current assets}}{\text{Current liabilities}}$$

$$\text{Return on equity} = \frac{\text{Net income}}{\text{Average total owner's equity}}$$

$$\text{Operating margin} = \frac{\text{Operating income}}{\text{Net sales}}$$

$$\text{Gross margin} = \frac{\text{Net sales} - \text{Cost of goods sold}}{\text{Net sales}}$$

$$\text{Inventory turnover} = \frac{\text{Cost of goods sold}}{\text{Average inventory}}$$

$$\text{Return on sales} = \frac{\text{Net income}}{\text{Net sales}}$$

$$\text{Asset turnover} = \frac{\text{Net sales}}{\text{Average total assets}}$$

$$\text{Return on assets} = \frac{\text{Net income}}{\text{Average total assets}}$$

$$\text{Long-term debt to capital} = \frac{\text{Long-term debt}}{\text{Long-term debt} + \text{owner's equity}}$$

---

[5]Occupancy costs include base rent, real estate taxes, common-area maintenance, building insurance, marketing/promotion funds, and percentage rent.

$$Receivable\ collection\ =\ \frac{Average\ accounts\ receivable}{Net\ sales/365\ days}$$

$$Revenue\ growth\ =\ \frac{This\ year's\ net\ sales\ -\ Last\ year's\ net\ sales}{Last\ year's\ net\ sales}$$

$$Gross\ margin\ =\ \frac{Net\ sales}{Net\ sales\ -\ Cost\ of\ sales}$$

Financial ratios are only meaningful when compared to an appropriate benchmark. Always compare ratios of firms in the same industry and only compare prior periods of the same firm if there have been no significant changes in its operations or policies. Accounting methods used for inventories and depreciation schedules can confound comparisons. Off-balance-sheet financing and inventory liquidations can also make analysis difficult. Although ratios can be improved, it may not be in the long-term best interests of the company to do so. For example, the current ratio can be improved or affected by transactions and accounting methods as follows:

By Transactions

Current assets = $200; current liabilities = $150: the current ratio = 1.33.

Use cash to pay $75 in accounts payable.

Current assets = $125; current liabilities = $75; current ratio = 1.67

The current ratio has improved, but liquidity has decreased.

By Accounting Method

XYZ Corporation reports current assets of $187 million and current liabilities of $154 million at the end of 1997, which resulted in a current ratio of 1.21.

In its footnotes, XYZ Corporation discloses that it uses the *last in, first out* (LIFO) accounting method[6] for its inventories and that the current value is $139 million more than its historical cost.

---

[6]Last in, first out (LIFO)—Accounting method which assumes that the inventory acquired most recently is sold (used up) first. First in, first out (FIFO) associates the most recent costs with inventories. LIFO provides a more realistic income picture because net income measured using LIFO combines current sales prices and current acquisition costs.

The current ratio does not take into account the true value of the inventory, resulting in a less desirable ratio that is not completely represented. Financial ratios for many industries are available from various publications, on-line database services, trade organizations, and the Internet. Some good sources include *Annual Statement Studies* (Robert Morris Associates), *Industry Norms and Key Business Ratios* (Dun and Bradstreet), *Standard & Poor's Industry Surveys, Value Line Investment Survey, Moody's Manuals,* and *The Retailing Industry Statistical Review* (First Chicago NBD & Arthur Andersen).

Summary

Understanding and using financial statements requires knowing how the basic components of financial reports are developed and used. It involves recognizing different reporting alternatives which can make interpretation difficult. Financial reports contain information that is:

- Objective and verifiable
- Subjective and manipulated.

Users of financial statements must be aware of the process by which reports are constructed. Financial statements should meet the needs of external users who cannot get information directly, and should be comprehensible to those who have a reasonable understanding of business and economic activities of the entity being reported on.

Financial statements are not designed to measure value, but they do provide helpful information to those who wish to estimate value and economic viability of an operating entity. They should help lenders, investors, landlords, creditors—and even nonfinancial professionals—assess the amounts, timing, and uncertainty of prospective cash receipts.

John Bell, CLS, is Senior Vice President, Hiffman Shaffer Associates, Inc., Chicago, Illinois.

3 | The Lease

John L. Gerdes, SCSM

The Basics of a Lease

Lease: A contract transferring the right to the possession and enjoyment of [property] for a definite period of time. The signed agreement between landlord and tenant that establishes responsibilities, sets standards, and states what is recoverable from tenants for the maintenance process.

Now that you know the formal definition of a *lease,* it is important to learn what it really means in the business of shopping centers. This grand legal document, which yields so much power in the industry, can be as short as one page or as long as one hundred pages; no matter what the size, the overall goal is to establish a relationship between the tenant and the landlord.

For the landlord, the goals include receiving reasonable rent, recovering expenses, enhancing value, and protecting the investment. The tenant's goals are similar, yet they operate from a different set of criteria. Therefore, lease negotiations between landlords and tenants present unique challenges and must be understood from each party's perspective.

ANALYZING A LEASE TO PREPARE BILLINGS

Assuming the lease is complete at this point, someone must review it and delineate all the items that will be billed to the tenant. Some of the basics are rent, common-area maintenance (CAM) charges, real estate taxes, and marketing fees. The items usually labeled "other" include insurance, HVAC (heating, ventilation, and air-conditioning), special assessments, and a myriad of possible charges specific to a particular center. Those charges must be reviewed and documented in some easily recoverable fashion for future use. Remember, there could be a change in accountants, managers, bookkeepers, or other personnel who have to review these charges. You do not want to have to review the entire lease document again. Therefore, when the lease is complete, create a *lease abstract*. This is a short version containing the most important facts about the lease.

PREPARING A LEASE ABSTRACT

The form in Exhibit A contains a tremendous amount of information, from square footage to tenant improvements, on a single page. There is even space for lease provisions, those items that are beyond the normal concessions made in lease negotiations. For example, perhaps the tenant demands that it be allowed to close on a particular day or stay open late for an after-hours St. Patrick's Day Party, or there may be a special clause allowing the tenant to have live animals within its leased premises. In any case, if it may cause concern, this is the place to make note of it.

CALCULATING RECOVERY OF EXPENSES

Keep in mind that you cannot charge the tenant until you figure out what the total amount for expenses is. Generally, during the leasing process, the amount of estimated charges for each particular area has been provided on either a square-foot or annual basis, so the tenant is aware of the approximate cost of operating at the center. The exact amount may not be known, however, until the actual bill is sent. The final bill may vary due to the actual expenses or actual leased square footage. A year-end reconciliation rectifies the difference.

COMMON-AREA MAINTENANCE (CAM)

The CAM cost is usually a big expense for both the landlord and the tenant. It is often the source of much negotiation during the leasing process, because each side tries to get the most beneficial possible payments. In general, the cost of operating the shopping center is divided by the total amount of square footage, resulting in the cost per square foot. If there is a total cost of $500,000 and 100,000 square

Exhibit A: Lease Abstract

Property:	Date:
Submitted by:	
☐ New lease　☐ Renewal　☐ Amendment	

Tenant

Legal name	DBA:
Contact name:	State of incorporation:
Address:	
Telephone number:	
Guarantor:	State of incorporation:
Full guarantee　☐ Guarantee limited to:	
Tenant notice address:	

Lease Provisions

Space No.:	Sq. ft.:	Frontage:

☐ Renewal/Relocation existing deal:	Space no.:	Sq. ft.:	Min. rent:	Effective rent:

Use:

Term	Years:	Months:	Opening date:	Expiration date:

Minimum annual rent budget:

Years:	Dollars/Sq. ft.	Dollars/Yr.	% Rent	☐ Natural ☐ Unnatural breakpoint

Department store increase:		

Security deposit:

Tenant allowance budget:

Cash to tenant:	$　/sq. ft.	$	
Abated rent:	$　/sq. ft.	$	
Abated extra charges:	$　/sq. ft.	$	
Recapture:	$　/sq. ft.	$	
Landlord's work:	$　/sq. ft.	$	
Brokerage commission:	$　/sq. ft.	$	%　　　☐L&B

☐ Outside broker

Total cost:	$　/sq. ft.	$

Ancillary charges

CAM	☐Full pro-rata $　/sq. ft.	☐ Other
Taxes	☐Full pro-rata $　/sq. ft.	☐ Other
Utilities:	HVAC　$ /sq. ft.	Electric　$　/sq. ft.
Marketing fund	$　/sq. ft.	Media fund　　$ /sq. ft.

Escalations	Initial marketing charge $	Special assessment

Construction chargebacks:

Special lease provisions:

feet of GLA (gross leasable area), the CAM cost is $5 per square foot. A typical CAM clause is shown next.

Exhibit B: CAM

SECTION 0.1—Tenant's proportionate share of the common-area charge, which shall be computed on the ratio that the floor area of the demised premises bears to the total floor area of the shopping center that is leased, occupied, and producing rent, including the demised premises, but *excluding* floor area the landlord designates as anchor tenant and/ or specialty store tenant space and space for recreational and convenience uses; provided, however, the tenant's share of the common-area charge shall be calculated on the basis of not less than 80 percent (80%) of the gross leasable area of the shopping center (excluding anchor tenant space, specialty store tenant space, and space for recreational and convenience uses).

SECTION 0.2—Common-Area Charge: "Common-area charge" means the landlord's gross actual costs and expenses of every kind or nature incurred by or imposed upon the landlord, in or by reason of the landlord's ownership, operation, management, maintenance, and/or replacement of the common areas, the cost of operating, repairing, heating, lighting, air-conditioning, cleaning, and painting; removing snow, ice, leaves, and debris; providing off-site parking; providing security; sewage and trash-disposal charges; insurance for hazards and other risks and any other insurance the landlord deems necessary; licensing fees; a reasonable allowance for the depreciation of, or for the rental of, vehicles and maintenance equipment; direct and payroll overhead, payroll taxes and benefits, and the cost of personnel to implement such services; and any other costs and expenses (except ground rent) that are allocable.

You will note that there are many areas listed in this clause that encompass all aspects of operating the center. It is ideal to protect your particular standard clause during negotiations. Alterations to any of the listed items that constitute the CAM charge will result in changes in the recovery from the tenant. Note that if a tenant excludes or includes something that is a variation from the norm, it will result in a separate calculation by the accounting department. What happens if the CAM charge is altered and you end up with several cost bases or cost centers for recovery? The result could be an accounting nightmare. What if the clause were different for every tenant in a 100-tenant shopping center? There would be one hundred different recovery calculations. Generally, this area is left alone for that reason. The tenant will seek other solutions, as will be discussed later.

REAL ESTATE TAXES (RET)

Usually the same system used for calculation of CAM is used here as well. Again, the landlord would certainly prefer to leave this expense as a straight pass-through without altering the clause in the lease. An example is shown below:

Exhibit C: Taxes

SECTION 0.3—Tenant's share of taxes shall be computed on the ratio that the floor area of the demised premises bears to the total floor area of the shopping center that is leased, occupied, and producing rent, including the demised premises but excluding floor area the landlord designates as anchor tenant space and/or specialty store tenant space, and floor area used for post office, child-care nursery purposes, or other uses principally for service, convenience, or recreation to customers of the shopping center (collectively, "recreational and convenience uses"); provided, however, the tenant's share of taxes shall be calculated on the basis of not less than 80 percent (80%) of the gross leasable area of the shopping center (excluding anchor tenant space, specialty store tenant space, and space for recreational and convenience uses).

As you see in Exhibit C, real estate taxes represent a significant portion of the expenses for the center. If they are carelessly negotiated, years later this will resurface as a decrease in value. The landlord has little control over the center's real estate taxes, as they are dictated by a government entity. Although every landlord reviews these costs carefully and hires tax consultants to lobby and protest, in the end, the taxes are what they are. The tax clause should remain intact so it can be fairly administered by everyone. If there are variations, refer back to the CAM discussion. Prepare for the nightmares and turnover in personnel that can result.

ADMINISTRATION FEE

The cost of actually administering the common area is a standard addition to the overall cost of CAM. The standard fee is 15 percent for CAM and 10 percent for taxes but is often negotiated. As you will see in the upcoming example, the loss of that fee is significant to value and cash flow. Although usually thought of as a CAM allocation, administrative charges for real estate taxes and insurance are common as well. In real estate taxes, a considerable amount of time and effort is spent individually, with legal counsel and consultants, to get the lowest possible value, which benefits both the owner and the tenants. Insurance can be a similar consideration, as there is considerable expense involved in researching insurance needs, costs, and coverages. "Admin. fees," as they are often called, can be heavily negotiated. While commonly accepted, at some rate, for CAM, such fees for taxes and insurance are more difficult to obtain.

PERCENTAGE RENT

The concept of *percentage rent,* referring to a percentage of the tenant's annual sales, has been a long-standing part of the shopping center industry. Many department stores have continued to lower their percentage rate over the years, as have many specialty tenants. In many ways percentage rent is the only real upside about leasing to some tenants. The standard clause is usually something like the following:

Exhibit D: Percentage Rent

SECTION 3.03—The term "gross sales" shall mean the total amount in dollars of the actual sales price, whether for cash, on credit, or both, of all sales of merchandise and services and all other receipts of business conducted in or from the demised premises, including all mail or telephone orders received or filled at the demised premises, all deposits not refunded to purchasers, orders taken, although said orders may be filled elsewhere, and sales by any sublessee, concessionaire, or licensee, or otherwise, in said demised premises. Each sale upon installment or credit shall be treated as a sale for the full price in the month during which such sale is made irrespective of the time when the tenant receives payment from its customer. No deduction shall be allowed for uncollected or uncollectible credit accounts. Gross sales shall not include any sums collected from the purchaser and paid out by the tenant to the taxing authority for any sales or excise tax imposed by any duly constituted governmental authority (however, any amount the tenant receives for collecting such taxes shall be included in the definition of gross sales), nor the exchange of merchandise between the stores of the tenant, if any, where such exchange of goods or merchandise is made solely for the convenient operation of the business of the tenant and not for the purpose of consummating a sale that has theretofore been made at, in, or from the demised premises or for the purpose of depriving the landlord of the benefit of the sale that otherwise would be made at, in, or from the demised premises, nor the amount of returns to shippers or manufacturers, nor the amount of any cash or credit refund made upon any sale where the merchandise sold, or some part thereof, is thereafter returned by the purchaser and accepted by the tenant, nor sales of fixtures which are not a part of the tenant's stock in trade. Gross sales shall be registered at the time each sale is made in cash registers, in accordance with good commercial practice.

The calculation is very simple. You take the amount of the annual base rent and divide it by the agreed-on percentage factor, thereby creating a *sales breakpoint,* often called a *natural breakpoint.* Theoretically, that is the point at which the tenant breaks even on expenses and sales and begins to make a profit or perhaps extra profit. The landlord should have a percentage of those sales because the landlord, again theoretically, had a lot to do with the success of the tenant in that particular center or location. The debate involves determining the correct percentage factor. The lease may be negotiated with a set sales hurdle that is not related to the above calculation. (That is usually referred to as an *unnatural breakpoint* and should be noted on the abstract.) Percentage rent is a big factor in value, particularly if the center is a high performer. An appraiser will review the percentage rent amounts and often add significant value to the center based on future percentage rent increases.

DEFINING THE LEASE YEAR

The significance of how the year is defined in the lease is important to your accounting system and to your ownership. If your company owns all its own real estate, the lease will be structured to fit its needs.

In some situations, the real estate is owned by another party. Then it is important to have the lease's defined year match the accounting year that the ownership requires. This is because it can be difficult to match a fiscal-year lease (which might be July to June) to a calendar-year budget or vice versa. The continued varying definition of a fiscal year, which can be basically any twelve-month period, adds more confusion to this area. The advice here is to try to match the lease year with your needs and thus to simplify your accounting and budgeting requirements.

Value Factors

Now that the basics of rent, CAM, real estate taxes, percentage rent, and the like have been discussed, it is important to evaluate their impact on the value of the shopping center.

IDEAL SHOPPING CENTER

By this point the landlord has argued and fought for all the lease clauses it thinks it deserves. Fortunately, the tenant agrees with all of the requests, including desired rent, full charges, administrative costs—the works. Remember, this is an example, so dreaming is allowed.

You will note that Table 3.1 sets the stage for an appropriately named ideal small shopping center, which is fully leased and maximized in value. The form explains the original cost, rent, CAM, real estate taxes, occupancy, and administrative recoveries. Remember, occasionally the landlord gets the right to recover a 15 percent administration fee on CAM and a 10 percent administration fee on taxes. That explains the ability to recover more than 100 percent of expenses. The excess over 100 percent actually is paying for the costs

Table 3.1   Ideal Shopping Center

Purchase Price $20,000,000   100,000 sq. ft.

Average rent/sq. ft. $20   CAM/sq. ft. $5   Real estate taxes/sq. ft. $3

100% occupied
CAM recovered at 115%
Taxes recovered at 110%

Gross rental revenue	$ 2,000,000
CAM	$ 500,000
Admin. fee	$ 75,000
Real estate taxes	$ 300,000
Admin. fee	$ 30,000
Total revenue	$ 2,905,000
Less CAM expense	$ 500,000
Less tax expense	$ 300,000
Net operating income (NOI)	$ 2,105,000
Cap rate	10%
Current value	$21,050,000
Return on NOI =	10.53%

the landlord incurs for administrative time spent reducing expenses of the tenants. It is an example of what can theoretically happen.

First add up all revenue items collected, to obtain a total revenue figure. Then deduct the expenses, to determine net operating income (NOI). Net operating income is the income realized after operating expenses have been deducted from *gross income* (total revenue). These operating expenses include property taxes, insurance, utilities, management fees, heating and cooling expenses, and repairs and maintenance fees. Basically, to determine the value, simply divide the NOI by the established cap rate, or capitalization rate, which is the rate used to convert income into value. In this case, the cap rate is 10 percent, making the calculation simple: the NOI here is 10 percent of the value. For a fully leased center such as this one, the cap rate actually would be substantially less; however, a more accurate rate of 8.75 percent or 9.25 percent (depending on the current market) would be more difficult to calculate. The principle is the same: the calculation—NOI divided by cap rate—sets the value.

In the more complex actual financial world, many other factors are used to determine value. A *pro forma*—estimates of costs and income—would be completed based upon growth rates and future cash flows discounted back at a reduced rate. (Cash flows constitute the projection of anticipated income and expenses according to the actual or anticipated times of receipt and disbursement.) In the ideal example, the NOI is simply divided by the original investment base (cost) to determine a return on NOI. A "cash on cash" return is calculated by dividing cash out by cash in. In this example there are no other deductions from NOI, so it equals cash flow. In a financial statement there are other deductions from NOI, such as debt service, before you end up with cash flow. Here the return on NOI and cash is 10.53 percent.

You have done well with this property by having a good return, an increase in value, and 100 percent occupancy. The owner is very happy! How could this picture be changed? What are the problems that will affect the value? A major factor is the lease form itself.

Lease Forms

GROSS LEASE

In the case of real estate leases, *gross* usually means that all the charges are lumped together in one sum, resulting in the amount the tenant is billed for. Usually a gross deal will not have any positive effects for the property. When gross charges are set up in a lease, the landlord has two choices. The first is to take all the gross charges as rent and apply them to revenue, which will increase net operating income. The second option is to allocate some portion of the gross rent to real estate taxes, common-area charges, and even marketing charges. Usually a gross rent will result in a lower overall package of rent and charges for the property. When CAM charges or real estate taxes get excessively high, tenants have a tendency to try to negotiate a gross rental, in hopes of eliminating future increases in occupancy costs.

If a decision is made to allocate a certain amount of gross rent to the separate charges, that amount should be at a reasonable rate. In fact, the landlord is likely to be legally bound to be fair in the allocation to ensure that a favorable deal for one tenant does not adversely affect another. In reality, recoveries in excess of 100 percent are rare. The alternative for the tenant is to require a cap on certain charges.

The summary in Table 3.2 clearly illustrates the effects of a gross

Table 3.2　Ideal Shopping Center

Purchase Price $20,000,000　　　　100,000 sq. ft.

Average rent/sq. ft. $20　　CAM/sq. ft. $5　　Real estate taxes/sq. ft. $3

100% occupied

50,000 sq. ft. gross @ $22 − 50,000 sq. ft. CAM recovered at 115%

Taxes recovered at 110%

Gross rental revenue	$ 2,100,000
CAM	$ 250,000
Admin. fee	$ 37,500
Real estate taxes	$ 150,000
Admin. fee	$ 15,000
Total revenue	$ 2,552,000
Less CAM expense	$ 500,000
Less tax expense	$ 300,000
Net operating income (NOI)	$ 1,752,500
Cap rate	10%
Current value	$17,525,000
Return on NOI =	8.76% Loss of $3,525,000 in value

lease on a shopping center. For this example, assume that half of the center has now been leased to a single tenant of 50,000 square feet with a $22 gross rental rate. If it is assumed from the lease that all of the gross rent is going to gross rental revenue, the effect is dramatic. CAM, real estate recoveries, and administrative costs are now cut in half while expenses remain the same. Although gross rental revenue has increased, it is not enough to offset the loss in CAM and taxes.

The loss in those revenues ($352,500) results in a reduction in value of $3,525,000, and the return on NOI has dropped to 8.76 percent. This could be a very serious problem if your return goals as an owner were based on the original 10.53 percent threshold. The other tenants would not be affected by accounting for the gross lease, because the landlord is absorbing the costs on an equitable basis.

TRIPLE NET LEASE

The most common lease form is called the *triple net lease,* which is one in which the tenant pays 100 percent of all taxes, insurance, and maintenance associated with a shopping center. Many years ago a standard was established to allow the landlord to recover the costs of operating the shopping center through the lease. Separate cost centers or cost bases for CAM, real estate taxes, and insurance provide direct pass-throughs that pay for most of the expenses of running the center.

There are administrative costs associated with each of these cost centers, which often may be recovered as well. Previously, the potential for 15 percent and 10 percent fees for CAM and taxes, respectively, were mentioned. The advantage of the triple net lease is that it allows the owner to operate the center in a first-class manner.

If the owner was totally responsible for all charges and thus repairs, the center might suffer over the long term. The decline of the physical aspect of the center is a problem, and increasing costs for maintenance are as well. This is a major concern for tenants who believe CAM charges have been increasing at an alarming rate in the last several years. Because retailers have little or no control over the common-area charges, they can become very suspicious of steadily increasing charges.

This is the main reason that gross leases and caps have become constant topics in lease negotiations. Real estate taxes are not as heavily debated, because taxes are set by a government entity over which neither the landlord nor the tenant usually has much control.

Though not directly related to the calculation of value, the charges for marketing the center are an important element in the center's operation. The efforts of the shopping center's marketing department are often hard to measure in exact dollars, but the failure of a center to be promoted properly and professionally can be reflected in falling sales and, subsequently, falling rents. The marketing charges may be in the form of a merchants association, a media fund, or a marketing fund. As these are maintained separately and do not transfer to the bottom line on a financial sheet, marketing is usually not considered in valuation.

Recovery Methods

As mentioned earlier, problems occur when company accountants have to calculate several different types of recoveries. An excess of different calculations can affect morale and even performance in the accounting department. It is best to avoid, or minimize, changes in recovery methods.

There are many ways of determining how recoveries are calculated. Basically, all the costs are divided by a predetermined area of square footage, and that amount is then assessed to each tenant on a per-square-foot basis. In the world of fractions, the amount of the expenses is the numerator and the square footage is the denominator. For example, if the cost is $500,000 and there are 100,000 square feet of GLA (gross leasable area), the CAM cost would be $5 per square foot. If you had a 1,000-square-foot store, you would pay $5,000 per year for your space. That seems easy enough if there were only one way to determine the amount of square feet in the dividing factor (denominator). Often an occupied percentage of GLA, such as 80 percent, is the standard for calculating cost or triggering special provisions in the lease. Below are examples of typical types of definitions for the dividers (denominators).

1. *Gross leasable area of a center.* This area is usually defined as the actual square footage that could be leased within the defined area of the shopping center. Some form of this is the most commonly used definition for the calculation of recoveries, particularly in smaller, anchorless centers.

2. *Leasable area of a center excluding anchors.* This is a simple way of taking the square footage of the anchors out of the calculation for the divider (denominator). In most cases, the anchor stores contribute little if anything to the expenses of the center. If the square footage of the anchors is left in, although they contribute at a lesser rate, the total recovery will be substantially less than expenses. The owner would be required to pay for any shortfall. In this definition, any contributions made by the anchors are usually taken off the expenses prior to the calculation of the rate per square foot. In the industry, everyone knows that major anchor stores usually negotiate an altered rate for recoveries, and both the tenant and owner use this clause to fairly determine recoveries. The administration fee is calculated on the total cost before any deductions, because the labor expense is an overall cost.

3. *Leased area of a center excluding anchors.* Although this definition is similar to the one above, the word *leased* changes the calculation for recovery. In the prior definitions, any space that is not leased during the year is still included in the calculation. The owner must ab-

sorb the costs for those vacant spaces, resulting in a decreased rate of recovery and decreased occupancy of the center. By this definition, not only the anchors but also the vacant space is excluded from the calculation for recoveries. This will result in a higher level of recovery of expenses as it is directly related to the amount of leased area. Tenants will object to this method, as they may feel it decreases the incentive for the owner to lease space. Obviously, however, the owner is losing rent in addition to the expenses on any vacant space, so the motivation to lease is still strong.

4. *Average leased area of a center excluding anchors.* This is the same as the definition above, except for an adjustment to the amount of the divider (denominator) at a predetermined time. Depending on the lease and the flexibility of your accounting system, the predetermined time may be at year's end, semiannually, or quarterly.

5. *Average open for business.* This is similar to the average leased clause but it further protects the owner, because the tenant actually has to be open for business to be included in the divider (denominator). In the event of a closing or bankruptcy, the space is technically leased and would be included in the calculations above. The likelihood of collection of expenses would be minimal in those situations. With average open for business, the owner would recalculate the divider and spread the costs.

As you can see, these clauses have a profound effect on value, similar to the earlier discussion of the effect of a gross lease on value. All of the clauses affect the rate of recovery and the owners' contribution, which in turn will affect value.

RECOVERY VARIATIONS

There are many ways to alter the above types of recovery methods, each with a specific purpose. The owner needs to be aware that each restriction in the calculation may limit the ability to collect full recoveries, which will affect both cash flow and value. The most common variation results from defining the excluded area.

> *Greater than xx,xxx square feet.* This clause is inserted to put a particular-sized tenant into a separate cost center. For example, the owner may want to lease 25,000 square feet to a tenant. Usually this tenant will not pay a full *pro rata* (exactly proportionate) charge, as an average tenant will. This clause, often called a spe-

cialty store exclusion, allows that the tenant be treated as an anchor. The tenant's contribution is deducted from the overall expenses before the calculation. The square footage is usually inserted as 15,000 square feet, and the tenant will often negotiate that square footage up to 50,000, restricting the options.

Tenant name specific. A new tenant may recognize a large user as a special exclusion and identify it by name.

Tenant name specific or a replacement. Considering the volatility of the market, the owner should always try to protect itself by getting a replacement clause. If the one tenant named vacates the space, the owner may forever be liable for the expense of the space despite having found a replacement.

Tenant name specific or a replacement tenant where the replacement exceeds xx,xxx square feet. Larger spaces—for example, 50,000 square feet—could be broken up into smaller ones. Protection will be sought to guarantee that any special exclusions apply only if the new tenant is of a certain size, if not a complete replacement.

Tenants not fronting on an enclosed mall. Spaces that have access only from the exterior are often excluded, as they do not benefit from many of the common charges. Usually these spaces have a lower rate based on only those expenses from which they actually benefit. For example, HVAC charges for the enclosed mall and interior landscaping might not be a part of the exterior tenant's charges. The owner should get the right to exclude those charges in the other tenants' leases, or the owner will pay for the difference in recovery.

Outparcels, theaters, specific buildings, basement space. All of these may come up in discussions about lease exclusions or variations for the purpose of recoveries. The owner needs to be very aware of the dangers of granting special requests to one tenant that may affect the recoveries of others.

Office space. Within a store, the space deemed as office is usually treated as regular leased space. Occasionally there are situations in which a regional office might function within a significant area of space. To lease the space, the owner may be willing to take a lesser rent and reduced charges. If that space is not excluded in other leases, the owner will bear some portion of that expense.

Mezzanine space. This is space built inside the leased premises, where there is enough room to build a second level. In many cases this space is charged to the tenant at full or half the rental rate of the regular space. Charges are usually discounted for the mezzanine space, and it is common to exclude such space from the recovery sections of the lease.

This list of exceptions could go on forever. In each center and each lease, there are many variations that will alter the recovery methods. The key is to be aware of the effects of changing these definitions. Value, cash flow, and or "the effectiveness of" your accounting staff are at stake!

RECOVERY INCOME

Administration fee applied to all expenses except x, y, *and* z. Sometimes the tenant will elect to pay only for certain items within the CAM definitions. Perhaps the tenant feels that security and HVAC are the only areas they should pay the charges on. The owner will have to decide if it wants to create another recovery model (cost basis) or fight for the complete package.

Excluding capital items. Many tenants will request that any capital items be excluded from CAM expenses. The tenant believes that by allowing the inclusion of this expense, the owner is able to put items into the CAM that the owner should pay for. Generally this can be worked out with proper discussions to alleviate the concerns of the tenant.

Capital items over $xxx,xxx must be amortized over x years. Assuming you have successfully negotiated the ability to include some capital items, your next concern will be limits and timing. Major capital expenditures are usually amortized over several years to lessen the impact on CAM costs. Often the tenant will want to specify an amount and a term to amortize. When negotiated properly, this clause will not cause a problem. Be aware that granting some special limit or time frame may result in yet another recovery method.

Obviously this is another area in which options are limitless. The best solution is to explain your position, understand the effect on value and cash flow, and try to leave this clause as it is written.

Caps

Many times, a tenant will avoid the negotiations involved in specific exclusions in CAM charges by getting a cap on the charges. A cap is simply a maximum amount that the tenant would pay, no matter what the pro rata charge would be. If the tenant is able to negotiate a cap, it is usually a set amount or a percentage of increase.

A tenant who wants to ensure that it does not get caught paying exorbitant fees in the future will insist on a cap. Either a fixed amount or a fixed percentage increase will allow the tenant to grow sales and occupancy costs in a pro forma model and determine what the profitability of a prospective store will be. In today's competitive market, caps are becoming more common. As in all other areas of lease negotiations, caps come in many forms other than simple over-all caps:

1. Cap on all expenses except for utilities. It is reasonable to assume that utility costs are difficult if not impossible to control.
2. Cap on all expenses except for utilities and snow removal. If utility rates are difficult to control, think about snow!
3. Cap on CAM and taxes together. This gets close to a gross deal, and we know how that affects ownership. A cap on taxes works the same as a cap on CAM.
4. Cap increases annually by the Consumer Price Index (CPI). A commonly accepted means of determining the annual increase, rather than a fixed amount or percentage. This method will be discussed later in this chapter.

In addition, many different combinations of the above may be applied to a particular lease. Although caps eliminate many of the negotiations on particular items, they usually result in another cost recovery calculation and potential accounting nightmare.

The tenant desires a cap to control expenses over the next several years; if not negotiated properly, however, the effect of a cap may be lost value and cash flow for the center.

In Table 3.3, the latest description of the Ideal Shopping Center, 50 percent of it has been leased to a tenant with a cap on CAM and taxes.

The results are very harmful. The cash return has dropped to 9.76 percent, and the overall value of the center has decreased by $1,525,000. The other unwritten problem with caps is the way they become common in your center. If you begin to give caps to some tenants, others will begin to ask for the same. Eventually the center may have a fixed amount of recovery expense while expenses con-

Table 3.3   Ideal Shopping Center

Purchase Price $20,000,000   100,000 sq. ft.

$20 Average rent per square foot $5 CAM per square foot
$3 Real Estate taxes per square foot

100% occupied
CAM recovered at 115%
Taxes recovered at 110%
(50,000 square feet capped at $4 CAM
and $2 RET, no admin. charge)

Gross rental revenue	$ 2,000,000
CAM	$ 450,000
Admin. fee	$ 37,500
Real estate taxes	$ 250,000
Admin. fee	$ 15,000
Total revenue	$ 2,752,500
Less CAM expense	$ 500,000
Less tax expense	$ 300,000
Net operating income (NOI)	$ 1,952,500
Cap rate	10%
Current value	$19,525,000
Return on NOI	= 9.76% Loss of $1,525,000 in value

tinue to grow. Such a situation will erode the value and future salability of the center.

Food Court CAM

The other variation in CAM payments is derived from the nature of the tenant's business. Food courts create a much higher cost for trash and labor. The amount of trash generated is not proportionate to the cost normally allocated to another tenant of the same size.

Additionally, the costs associated with keeping the food court clean, picking up trays, cleaning tables, and so on are generally charged directly to those tenants. As a result, food court tenants pay an additional amount to cover these costs. These extra payments take many forms:

1. *Tenants pay some multiple of the standard CAM rate.* Often this is 50 percent to 100 percent more than the standard CAM.

2. *Tenants pay x percent of sales as food court CAM.* Assuming that individual tenants with higher sales generate more trash and labor expense, they pay a higher amount.

3. *Tenants pay a pro rata of the food court CAM based upon total sales.* The total costs of operating the food court are estimated at the beginning of the year, along with sales projections for the tenants. Food court tenants are then assessed their respective share. A year-end adjustment converts the estimates to fact.

4. *Tenants pay food court CAM.* Fifty percent pro rata based upon square footage and 50 percent pro rata based upon sales.

5. Include costs in CAM and deduct contributions. This may simplify the accounting for these costs and can be a reasonable solution. This practice may, however, lead to questions from other tenants if any special allocations are made to specific food court tenants.

This expense must be allocated properly to offset the costs and keep the CAM costs fairly dispersed throughout the center.

Consumer Price Index (CPI) Tables

As mentioned earlier, the *Consumer Price Index (CPI)* is an indicator of rising prices or inflation used to measure the impact on consumers. The U.S. Bureau of Labor Statistics publishes this information at the end of every month. CPI tables can be used to determine many increases in charges. Although they are most commonly used in marketing charges, they are often used in determining rent and CAM as well. The increase is calculated by taking the year of commencement (or any year negotiated) and making it a base year. Then the difference between the base year and current year becomes the multiplier to increase the charge.

Tenant Improvement Allowances

In today's leasing world, *tenant improvement allowances* (TIs or TAs) have become very common. Not too long ago, they were the exception

Table 3.4   Consumer Price Index Tables

1st Year	Jan	Feb	Mar	Apr	May	June	July	Aug	Sept	Oct	Nov	Dec	Jan
1913	9.8	9.8	9.8	9.8	9.7	9.8	9.9	9.9	10	10	10.1	10	9.9
1995	150.3	150.9	151.4	151.9	152.2	152.5	152.5	152.9	149.4	149.5	149.7	149.7	148.2
1996	154.4	154.9	155.7	156.3	156.6	156.7	157	157.3	153.2	153.7	153.6	153.5	152.4
1997	159.1	159.6	160	160.2	160.1	160.3	160.5	160.8	157.8	158.3	158.6	158.6	156.9
1998	161.6	161.9	162.2	162.5	162.8	163	163.2	163.4	161.2	161.6	161.5	161.3	160.5
1999	164.3												

rather than the rule. In some of the strong centers, it is still possible to complete deals without significant allowances, but this does not happen often. The amount of these expenditures directly affects the cash flow, return, and value of the center. In financial statements they are usually listed as part of the capital expenditures, below the line for net operating income.

As an alternative to offering a TI, some owners prefer to offer free rent. Keep in mind that there is really no such thing as free rent. One way or another, the ownership pays for that. However, if ownership does not have the cash necessary to fund TIs, free rent is a viable alternative.

A tenant who requests a $50,000 TI with a monthly rent of $10,000 might accept five months of free rent as an alternative. When granting free rent, you should be aware of the effect on NOI. (Obviously there needs to be a clarification that the tenant is getting free rent but not extra charges.) In that way the owner loses only rental revenue and not recoveries as well. Depending on the CAM allocation, the charges may start with the opening of the store instead of with the commencement of rental payments. The owner would then have to make up for the extra charges in addition to the loss of rental income.

Assuming the same $50,000 mentioned above as an example, that is exactly what would come off the net operating income and cash flow. Using the previous models, that $50,000 could be capped at (divided by) a rate of 10 percent, affecting the value by $500,000. Although concern for the owner's needs is always the primary motivation for making any lease deal, the change in the management fee, when free rent is applied, should also be understood. Again using the $50,000 figure, which is deducted from the NOI, the management fee is reduced accordingly. Assuming a 4 percent management fee, that reduction costs the management company $2,000.

Creating Value in a Lease

There are many other factors to consider within the lease document that can directly affect value but are often overlooked.

Getting the right to relocate. There may be an occasion when relocating an existing tenant may improve the overall value of the center. If the right tenant is available and willing to pay enough rent to justify the move, it would be a disservice to the ownership not to do it. More importantly, the opportunity for a center expansion, at some later date, might significantly increase the value of the center. A tenant in the way of such a major center event could become a costly hindrance without a relocation clause such as the one shown in Exhibit E.

Exhibit E: Relocation

SECTION 0.3   Relocation and Redevelopment of Shopping Center

(a) Tenant agrees that in the event of any redevelopment of the shopping center, the landlord shall have the right to require the tenant to relocate to another space in the shopping center. The landlord shall serve upon the tenant a written notice of relocation specifying a date (the relocation date) at least sixty (60) days from the date of such notice upon which such relocation is to take place. The tenant shall then have the right to relocate to a mutually agreeable space (the relocation premises). If, in the opinion of the tenant, a suitable location does not become available on or before the relocation date, the tenant shall have the right to cancel this lease as of the relocation date.

(b) If, in response to the landlord's notice, the tenant relocates to the relocation premises, all rent and other charges under this lease shall abate during any period in which the tenant is not open in any location and recommence on the earlier to occur of (i) the date on which the tenant actually opens the relocation premises for business; of (ii) a date sixty (60) days following the date on which the landlord makes the relocation premises available to the tenant.

(c) In the event of relocation as provided in this section, the landlord shall reimburse the tenant for the unamortized cost of tenant improvements to the demised premises, less any allowance given by the landlord. Unamortized cost shall be computed by using straight-line depreciation, with the life of improvements being the primary term of the lease.

Getting percentage rent. The calculation process for percentage rent has already been discussed. Realistic percentages and breakpoints will provide increasing income in future years, as the center and each particular tenant's sales level grow.

Limiting the number of deductions or exclusions from sales. The more exclusions are allowed, the more difficult the calculation is and the lower the percentage rent.

Eliminating or limiting options. Options are never to the advantage of the owner. In the world of appraised value, options will not carry the value of the actual term of the lease. It will be up to the appraiser to decide if that option will be exercised and the lease value included in future value calculations. Even mutual options are not a positive. If an option period is granted, it should include an option for the landlord to cancel if sales are not at a particular level. The center may have increased in desirability and productivity to a point where a particular tenant does not fit the tenant mix when the renewal option occurs.

Limiting the number of exclusives. Besides being a problem to keep track of, exclusives cause problems with legal interpretations. When certain categories become popular, the center is limited in taking advantage of the latest merchandise mix if it is restricted by exclusives.

Operating covenants. Many prospective tenants will ask about major tenants' or anchors' operating covenants, as they consider whether they will move to a particular center. Items covered in the operating covenants include a guarantee that all stores will be open during the same hours and on the same days. To maintain the future value of the center, a strong operating covenant such as the one in Exhibit F is a necessity.

Exhibit F: Continuous Operation

Section 1.1   Except when, and to the extent that, the demised premises may be untenantable by reason of damage by fire or other casualty, the tenant shall: (a) continuously and uninterruptedly use, occupy, operate, and conduct its business in the entire demised premises using its best efforts to produce the maximum volume of gross sales and to help establish and maintain a high reputation for the whole shopping center; (b) unless prohibited by law or required by the landlord to close, open for business each day (except Sundays) at 10:00 A.M. at the latest and remain open for business until 10:00 P.M. at the earliest, and further hours as may be designated by the landlord from time to time; (c) open for business on Sundays from 10:00 A.M. until 6:00 P.M. or at such other hours as the landlord shall designate from time to time; and (d) open for business on holidays at times as the landlord shall designate from time to time. Notwithstanding the foregoing, if the tenant's business is controlled by governmental regulations, the hours of operation prescribed by such governmental regulations shall apply. The tenant shall keep its store fully staffed continuously, and fully stocked with salable seasonal merchandise of merchantable quality and otherwise appropriate to the permitted uses. Failure on the tenant's part to comply with this section shall result in an assessment of five hundred and no/100 dollars ($500.00) per day.

Having the right to buy out a tenant (especially an anchor) if the tenant ceases operations. A vacant space still under lease may be providing income, but it is still a detriment to the center. If it is an anchor space, the effect can be very harmful. The right to recover that space at some price is essential to the future of the center. Failure to open for business is usually defined as a default. Upon notice of the default, the legal process is in place to recover the space vacated, and so the recovery clause, like the one in Exhibit G, becomes invaluable.

Exhibit G: Recovery

SECTION 1.2   Landlord's recovery. If the tenant's right to possession of the demised premises is terminated or if the term of this lease expires or is terminated, the landlord may immediately or at any time thereafter change the locks of the demised premises and/or enter the demised premises and remove the tenant, tenant's agents, and subtenants, and any invitees, and any of its or their property from the demised premises, and the landlord may repossess and enjoy the demised premises.

Requesting that anchors make voluntary contributions to promotion funds. Though seldom achieved, it never hurts to ask for such a contribution. The marketing team will need to provide some amount of documentation of the value of their function.

The importance of commencement-date letters. Debate can occur as to when charges actually begin. Sending out a letter to document the date can eliminate questions regarding when the lease begins and when the term is over.

Most favored nations. Some tenants, particularly anchors, will request this clause. It simply means that whatever concessions, caps, or other benefits are given to any other tenant must be given to them as well. Before granting such a clause, think about the long-term future of your center. These clauses are truly an accounting and leasing nightmare. The granting of one concession could result in alterations to any lease with that clause.

Property Management Software

There are many types of software in the market. As you explore them, keep in mind the diverse things discussed in this chapter. For the sake of the accounting folks and your own sanity as well, make sure the software does the functions you need and can be understood by everyone within your firm. If you are a fee manager, compatibility with other types of software will also be a major concern.

In closing, it should be apparent that many of the clauses in the lease have direct effects on the value of the center. Understanding how these clauses work will make manipulation of them easier and less costly. The ownership, landlord, and tenant are partners in the success of the center, and the lease is a partnership agreement. It is hoped that everyone can achieve a profitable outcome when the document is fully understood.

John L. Gerdes, SCSM, is Director of Retail Properties at L&B Realty Advisors Inc., Dallas, Texas.

Kate M. Sheehy

The Business Plan

A *business plan* is a road map for the operation of a shopping center for the upcoming year or years. The business plan sets a direction and destination (strategy) for the center and plots the course (tactics) to get there.

The preparation of the business plan involves all members of the shopping center's team: property management, operations, leasing, marketing, tenant coordination, development, and accounting. In many organizations, input is also necessary from various corporate functions such as payroll, information systems, and legal support. Generally this input takes the form of expenses charged or allocated to the shopping center.

Like any team, the business plan team needs a captain or, using the road-map analogy, a driver. This responsibility usually belongs to the businessperson most directly accountable for the performance of the shopping center and the accomplishment of the business plan's objectives. Most often this is the property's general manager.

One school of thought about shopping center business plans is that they really comprise two parts. The first is the operating budget, which tends to be for the upcoming year; the second is the strategic plan for the shopping center asset, which has a longer time frame, usually three to five years. The phrase *business plan* has come to be used interchangeably to describe each part. For purposes of this discussion, ''budget'' will describe the one-year operating budget; ''business plan" will describe the entire package presented to ownership for approval—including the budget.

The Business Plan Summary

A good business plan needs a great executive summary. One approach to writing an executive summary is to assume that the owner's representative is going to read only this part of the plan. Therefore, the summary must communicate everything the owner's representative needs to know in order to secure approval. This assumption forces great discipline on the business plan team to explain concisely how the property will meet the owner's objectives in the budget year.

When a journalist writes an article, he or she must answer six questions: Who? What? Where? When? Why? and How? Using these questions as prompts, an executive summary for a business plan could be designed this way:

Who? Identify the ownership, asset management, and property management (and sometimes the lender, too) for the shopping center. They constitute the audience for the business plan. This may also be the most appropriate place to describe the owner's objectives for the property, including investment return expectations and the hold or sell strategy. Identify any lender requirements as well.

What? Describe the property, its anchor stores, its size, and its location.

Where? Describe the center's market, the demographics, and the competition. Focus particularly on changes in conditions and how those changes are affecting or may affect the shopping center.

When? Describe the targets for the budget year: occupancy, rent, sales, net operating income (NOI), and accounts receivable. Compare these targets to the forecast for the current year and actual results for the prior year.

Why? Describe the situation(s) driving the rate of growth (or decrease) for the budget year compared to those of the current year. Draw upon the analysis of the market and competition to support the targets. Discuss the leasing environment, including vacancies, renewals, lease expirations, and potential unscheduled store closings. Explain nonrecurring items such as early lease termination payments received in the current year and not anticipated in the budget year.

How? Describe the capital plan for the center. Even if the operating budget is for only one year, the capital plan will probably be for three to five years. Include tenant allowances and other leasing related costs. Support requests for other capital with the description of the center already provided and/or the analysis of the market and competition.

The development or redevelopment outlook for the property is also part of the business plan. This may be part of the capital plan or have its own section in the summary.

Explain, too, how the plan for the center will increase its value and maximize the return on the owner's investment in the property.

The business plan will include a section providing detailed support for each part of the executive summary.

The Operating Budget

The operating budget projects the center's financial performance for the next year. In the broadest terms, the operating budget is a prediction of what the operating statement, also called an income statement or profit-and-loss statment, will look like at the end of the year. An operating statement is a financial statement showing revenues earned by the business, the expenses incurred in earning the revenues, and the resulting net income or loss. The accounting method used to prepare financial statements for the property will influence the budgeting process—particularly in recognizing the timing of events.

The cash basis method of accounting recognizes revenues and expenses as they are received or paid. A budget prepared on this basis would schedule percentage rent revenues as the landlord receives them. Percentage rent is any rent based upon a percentage of the tenant's gross sales; *overage rent* is percentage rent paid on gross sales exceeding a breakpoint, or break-even point. In a cash basis budget, because tenants tend to exceed breakpoint during the holiday season, the timing of overage rent receipts would probably be heavily weighted toward the end or the beginning of the year. In the cash method, real estate tax and insurance expenses would be scheduled in the month they are due to be paid.

If the shopping center is encumbered with debt, and the financial statements for the property record the payments on the loan, the budget should include the loan payments too. These payments will comprise principal and interest, as required by the loan terms. In a cash basis budget, capital expenditures should be planned for each month that a payment is expected to be made. For example, if a tenant allowance is payable when a tenant completes its store build-out, the allowance should be budgeted in the same month the store is expected to open.

The accrual basis method of accounting recognizes revenues and expenses as they are earned or payable, regardless of when they are actually received or paid. A budget prepared on this basis may recognize percentage rents in each month of the year. Some management companies choose to recognize each month's percentage rent in the same proportion as the percentage of the year's sales are expected in each month. For instance, if a tenant was going to pay $100,000 in overage rent for the year, the January budget might be $5,500, because January's sales are typically about 5.5 percent of the retail year. In the accrual method, taxes and insurance would be budgeted in equal amounts during every month of the year.

In an accrual basis budget, the loan payments are recorded in two parts: the principal portion reduces the amount of the loan on the balance sheet, and the interest portion is an expense. Using the accrual method, capital expenditures are recorded in the month the service is performed or the material(s) delivered.

The first page of the operating budget will be a summary, in operating statement format, of the revenues and expenses for the budget year. This summary will usually include a comparison to the current year's budget and/or forecast and one or more prior year's actual results. An example of a summary is attached as Exhibit I on page 150.

RENT AND OCCUPANCY

Without a doubt, rent is the most important component of a shopping center's revenues. Therefore, the leasing portion of the business plan and the budget is absolutely critical. The first step in the preparation of the business plan and budget is the development of the leasing assumptions. Many people prefer a format for leasing assumptions that includes all the spaces in the shopping center categorized as occupied or vacant. The occupied component is subdivided into stores:

- Expected to remain occupied in the budget year
- Whose leases will expire but are expected to renew
- Whose leases will expire but will not renew
- That may close before the lease termination date.

Vacant space, unscheduled closings, and all expirations are treated as the inventory of space available for the budget year.

Once this inventory has been developed, the leasing representative and general manager will complete the assumptions for that space:

- Retailer and/or merchandise category
- Opening date and rent over the term of the lease
- Overage rent breakpoint and anticipated first-year sales
- Common-area maintenance (CAM) and all other charges
- Tenant allowance and any cost for landlord work.

Careful attention should be given to budgeting opening dates for new leases. Overly aggressive timing can result in unfavorable variances in financial performance. Consideration should be given to retailers' preferences for opening new stores, which correlate to peak merchandising periods.

In addition, assumptions about the timetable, from striking a deal with a tenant to building a store, should be reasonable based on the property's history or that of the leasing organization. For instance, assume that it takes an average of ninety days to get a store open once the lease is signed. A new tenant probably should not be budgeted to open on May 1 if the prior tenant will not vacate the space until March 30. An exception might be when a space is so clean that the replacement tenant can move right in.

From this set of assumptions, the next step is to create an occupancy schedule by month and to calculate average occupancy for the budget year. Average occupancy is a leading indicator for rent revenue and net operating income (NOI). Net operating income is the difference between the operating revenues and expenses of the business. If the average occupancy based on the initial budget leasing assumptions is lower than the average occupany projected for the current year, NOI is likely to be lower as well. Without extenuating circumstances, ownership may find that unacceptable. If that is the case, the leasing assumptions should be revised before additional effort is invested in the revenue side of the budget.

Once the average occupancy is agreed on, revenue schedules can be prepared for rent and all charges. In many shopping centers, particularly regional malls, there is a 1:1 relationship between rent and NOI. For that reason, budgeted rent schedules are very detailed, identifying the amount due from each tenant in each month. *Rent steps* are budgeted in the appropriate month. Rent steps are the scheduled increases in rent specified in a tenant's lease. Although creating detailed schedules may seem burdensome, having them will make it easier to analyze performance variances during the upcoming year.

There is a reasonableness test that can be used to check if rent has been calculated correctly in the budget:

1. Calculate the difference between the budget year's rent and the current year's forecasted rent. This is your total change in rent.

2. Subtract from that result any step rent increases in the budget year. This should be your net change in rent resulting from the leasing assumptions. (You may have to adjust the forecast year too, if there are large step rental increases in the latter part of the year. For instance, if there were step rentals effective in November that increased 1997 NOI by $15,000, their effect in 1998 for twelve months would be $90,000.)

3. Calculate the change (in square feet) in average occupancy between the budget year and the current year's forecast. This is your total change in average occupancy.

4. Divide the change in rent, net of step increases, by the change in occupancy. The result is the average rent for the budget year's change in occupancy.

5. If this result is close to the shopping center's average rents or the average of rents for recent deals, the reasonableness test is met. If not, the numbers may bear some reexamination to check accuracy.

A word of warning: The tenants in the rent schedule must be the same tenants in the average occupancy schedule. If an anchor is not counted in occupancy but is counted in rent, the numbers will be skewed.

EXPIRATIONS

Although the leasing assumptions for the budget include the expirations for the budget year, most business plans will include a schedule outlining the expiration dates of all the leases in the center. Such a schedule helps to identify both risk and opportunity. Exhibit VI on page 155 is an example of a lease expiration summary.

If a shopping center is not performing well, having a large number of tenant leases expire represents risk. On the other hand, if the center is very successful and particularly if there is an opportunity for redevelopment or expansion, big lease turnover represents opportunity to remerchandise and create value.

If the business plan is used as a basis for the property's appraisal, it is important to address the risk and opportunity represented by the lease expiration schedule. The appraisal should use reasonable assumptions for retention, downtime, and particularly new rental rates.

The completed business plan will set forth targets for leasing during the budget year. Because many leases expire on either December 31 or January 31, they may be overlooked in creating objectives for leasing. A leasing representative's goal for any year should include the execution for renewals for leases expiring at the end of the budget year.

Completing the plan for renewals ensures that all tenants who do not plan to renew are identified and that the inventory of available space is accurately counted. This may seem insignificant, but the downtime between the expiration of one lease and the replacement with another store can create unexpected cash shortfalls. In addition, if the leases for tenants who do renew are not executed in a timely fashion, the new rents and other terms will not be in place as the new year begins. This will create cash shortfalls, although the variance is a matter of timing.

SALES

There are a couple of ways to approach budgeting tenant sales. The most traditional is to predict the store sales for each tenant in the shopping center based upon its prior year and/or current year-to-date performance. Note that all tenants are included, whether or not they are currently paying percentage or overage rent. A second method, especially for centers in stable markets with relatively small changes in occupancy or tenant mix, is to budget sales by applying one growth-rate factor to all the sales in the center.

A hybrid approach, something between these two methods, is to use one growth factor for all tenants except the largest payers of percentage rents. As an example, say you have a 300,000-square-foot center with 90 percent occupancy and only 13,000 square feet of space expiring in the budget year. The rate of inflation, as measured by the Consumer Price Index (CPI) published by the U.S. Bureau of Labor Statistics, is expected to be 2 percent for the budget year. Because this center's growth has generally been higher than CPI, you choose to budget the sales for all tenants in the center to be 3 percent higher than the current year.

This year's overage rent is projected to be $100,000. One jewelry store pays $40,000 of that total. The leasing plan calls for another jewelry store to be added to the merchandise mix. The existing jewelry store represents a significant portion of the total overage rent, and you want to avoid overstating the budget. You anticipate that the store's sales will be flat, given the new competition in the center. Therefore, you do not budget a sales increase for the existing store.

Sales drive rents, and in appraisals, sales affect the rental rates anticipated for future years. In a shopping center owned by an entity that restates market value each year, ownership may be reluctant to use any global assumptions for budgeting the upcoming year's sales. The sensitivity of the center's value to sales and, therefore, to rents may be too great.

To illustrate the point, say you have a 300,000-square-foot shopping center budgeted to be 90 percent occupied by the end of the budget year after renewing or remerchandising 65,000 square feet in lease terminations and adding 15,000 square feet of new stores. If current sales are $250 per square foot and you budget a 3 percent increase in the budget year and in the years thereafter, sales five years forward would be estimated at $290 per square foot. If the rent-to-sales ratio were 8 percent, the appraisal would probably use a market rent of $23 per square foot.

What happens if all the new and renewing tenants are projected to perform at an average of $275 per square foot and are expected to increase at 4 percent per year? (Assume that the rest of the center average $250 per square foot and increases at 3 percent per year.)

190,000	square feet × $290	=	$55,100,000
	($250 increased at 3% for 5 years)		
80,000	square feet × $335	=	26,800,000
	($275 increased at 4% for 5 years)		
270,000	square feet		$81,900,000
		divided by	270,000 square feet
			$303.00 per square foot

In five years, the center's sales per square foot are expected to be $13 per square foot higher than the original estimate. Using the rent-to-sales ratio of 8 percent, the appraisal would probably use a market rent of $24 per square foot—$1 more than the original estimate. If the appraisal used a capitalization rate of 10 percent, every extra $1 of rent would be worth $10 in value. Capitalized value is calculated by dividing the cash flow or net operating income by a capitalization rate (cap rate). A cap rate is the ratio of income to price. (This is discussed again in chapter 6, "Understanding Rates of Return.")

It is the relationship of sales to rents that makes budgeting sales such an important part of the business process. To determine the right level of detail for sales forecasting, the budget team should confirm who will be using the business plan and for what purposes.

EXPENSES

Before you tackle the expense side of the budget, the methodology should be clear. Many owners and asset managers are asking for zero-based budgets. *Zero-based budgeting* is a method of developing a budget without basing it on any previous year's budgets; the starting point for each item is zero. If this is the approach for a property, instead of using a growth factor to increase the current year's expenses, the requirements for next year's operation must be defined, contracts rebid, and other research performed.

For instance, in a zero-based budgeting environment, traffic counts and incident reports for the last twelve months should be reviewed to determine the number of security hours needed for each day of the week, for shopping center hours and for hours the center is closed. Changes in conditions in the market or upcoming events and marketing activities should also be considered. Once management has determined the requirement, and where there is a third-party contractor, the contract can be rebid. When the contractor is selected, that bid becomes the budgeted expense.

Zero-based budgeting requires discipline and planning. It cannot be done overnight or "on the back of a napkin." It does, however, help to make management accountable for each dollar spent.

Ownership will require that a separate expense section be provided for owner's expense, that is, expense not recoverable from the tenants in CAM, real estate taxes, and other add-on charges. In identifying ownership's direct expense exposure, this section must include whatever analysis and explanation is necessary to demonstrate that these expenses support the investment objectives for the property. If such a section is required, it is likely that a detailed schedule of all fees paid to the management company will be included.

RECOVERIES

Many operating budgets include schedules that list what each tenant will pay for CAM, real estate taxes, and other charges. Most leases read that the tenant's share will be calculated by multiplying some expense number by a fraction. The numerator of the fraction is the tenant's area, and the denominator is the leasable area as defined in the lease. This calculation results in the annual amount due from the tenant.

Although billings or even budgeting may be done this way, many organizations rely instead on rate calculations in their budgets or business plans. *Rates* are the tenant's share of add-on charges stated on a per-square-foot basis. The rate is calculated by dividing some expense number by the leasable area denominator as defined in the lease.

For instance, in one lease clause a tenant might be budgeted to pay $5.00 per square foot based on the expenses (plus a 15 percent administration fee) and occupancy assumptions if the denominator in the lease is occupied gross leasable area (GLA). In the same center, however, a tenant might pay only $4.35 per square foot with a GLA denominator.

Calculating rates on a square-foot basis may not be essential to budgeting tenant revenue as long as the sum of all tenants' annual charges is calculated. Rates, however, are important to the leasing people so that they can quote an estimated occupancy cost to prospective tenants. For that reason, the rates calculated for CAM, real estate taxes, and other changes based on budgeted expense and budgeted occupancy are often called *quote rates*.

Revenue from tenants for CAM or other charges can be estimated without calculating either rates or individual tenant amounts by using *recovery ratios.* A recovery ratio is the relationship between related revenue and expense. This methodology is a high-level macro approach that is used less for budgeting and more as a reasonability test.

Say the standard lease for a shopping center states that the tenants' share of CAM is based on occupied area. If all the tenants signed that lease form, the landlord would recover all CAM expense regardless of occupancy. That would be 100 percent recovery. If calculating the tenant's CAM liabilities included a 15 percent administration fee and all the tenants signed the standard lease form, the landlord would recover all CAM expense plus the administration fee, for a 115 percent recovery. If you knew that recovery was 115 percent, you could calculate revenue by multiplying expense by 115 percent, or 1.15. If expense were $1 million, revenue would be $1,150,000.

It is hard to imagine a shopping center where all the tenants signed the same lease clause provisions, however, and equally hard to imagine the center with 100 percent recovery. Because of the diversity of lease language in any center, recovery will be something less than 100 percent.

So say instead that the budget team calculated each tenant's CAM share and has calculated total CAM revenue for the budget year to be $1,070,000 compared to expenses of $1 million. That is 107 percent recovery. What if the recovery rate for the current year is 110 percent? How do you explain the erosion between years? Do the leasing plans include assumptions for a large space user to execute a lease in which the CAM is capped at a level well below that of the standard lease? Or could there be an error in the calculations? Recovery ratio calculations and trend analysis can help to flush out mistakes in the revenue numbers.

THE BOTTOM LINE

This is the first line anyone looks at, so it is essential to understand what is being measured in the budget's bottom line. Net operating income (NOI) is the difference between revenue and expense, sometimes called profit (or loss). NOI is said to be before interest expense and depreciation if those items are not included in expense. Revenue, and therefore NOI, may exclude interest income as well.

Real estate investment trusts (REITs) use a measurement called funds from operations, or FFO. FFO is analogous to NOI. FFO equals net income (computed in accordance with generally accepted accounting principles), excluding gains (or losses) from debt restructuring and sales of property, plus depreciation and amortization after adjustments for unconsolidated partnerships and joint ventures.

When the financial statements and budget are prepared on a cash basis, the bottom line will be net cash flow. Cash flow is the amount of spendable income available after all payments have been made for operating expenses and mortgage principal and interest.

Capital Expenditures

Capital expenditures are recorded as assets on the balance sheet, which is a financial statement showing a company's financial position at a particular point in time. Assets are the things a business owns and uses to operate the business. Assets have a useful life greater than a year; that is, their value to the business spans two or more years.

The largest class of capital expenditures in a shopping center's business plan is probably leasing related. Tenant allowances, landlord work to improve space, and commissions paid to the broker or management company are generally budgeted as capital expenditures. The costs incurred to lease space are amortized over the life of the lease(s) to which they are related.

Capital expenditures may represent either new assets or value added to existing assets. For example, a utility vehicle purchased (not leased) for housekeeping and maintenance might be a capital expenditure. If a snowplow blade for the vehicle was purchased the next year, it may also be a capital expenditure. The blade certainly expands the value of the vehicle, but it might not pass a materiality test. Each organization has certain dollar thresholds for what it capitalizes. The cost of the snowplow blade might not be enough to warrant capitalization in some companies.

Besides equipment such as the vehicle, capital expenditures include additions or changes to the building structure or to other property. Examples might be adding skylights to the building or expanding a storm sewer system. Determining whether an expenditure can be included in the cost pool for CAM or some other add-on charge may influence how ownership treats the expenditure in the budget.

For example, a shopping center owner may be required to make modifications to the public restrooms to comply with ADA (Americans with Disabilities Act). The shopping center leases allow that CAM expense may include expenditures necessary to comply with government regulations. Even though the restroom modifications might pass every test for capitalization, they might be budgeted as current year expense because of the impact of the lease language.

So the center's leases may affect decisions about capitalization as much as do generally accepted accounting principles. For that reason, some organizations include a section in the business plan to describe all major expenditures. The section is often divided into expense and capital items. Including both helps ownership to understand all the significant expenditures for the year, regardless of the accounting treatment.

Monitoring the Business Plan

If the objectives and targets of the business plan are to be achieved, then performance against the plan has to be monitored. One way to check performance is to compare year-to-date actual results against the plan. That comparison is limited, however, in that it may be affected by timing and may not adequately indicate whether full-year performance will meet the plan.

Many organizations update their budgets by forecasting year-end results based on both actual year-to-date activity and changes in conditions affecting the assumptions used to construct the budget. Such updating can be done as often as monthly but usually not less than quarterly. The purpose of forecasting is to tell management whether the property is on track to meet goals. If it is off track, the forecast alerts management to step up its revenue-creating efforts or modify its spending.

A forecast that is a call to action must explain why targets are not being met so that activity can be redirected. As an example, say you have a center that is forecast to be $120,000 short of budgeted NOI. Here are some possible variance explanations:

- "NOI will be down because revenue is less than budget."
- "NOI will be down due to lower rents."

- "NOI will be down because average occupancy is down 1.5 percent."

Not one of these statements tells exactly what happened or suggests what to do to fix the problem. Here is another way this explanation might have been written:

NOI will be down because the children's clothing store filed bankruptcy and rejected its lease ($36,000); the sporting goods store (5,000 square feet) opening in August is negotiating a gross lease at 8 percent of sales instead of the budgeted $20-per-square-foot minimum rent ($30,000); three store openings budgeted for April have been delayed until November ($77,000). These unfavorable variances are offset by the picture and framing store budgeted to close in February but now expected to operate all year ($23,000).

This last explanation is specific and detailed. It tells management that the children's store vacancy and possibly the seven months' delay for three stores offer some specialty leasing, or temporary, opportunities. It may also focus management's efforts on what might be done to get the three stores open before November. If the gross lease has not yet been executed, and this variance was not calculated earlier, management may ask the leasing representative to negotiate for a higher percentage or some other change in terms.

The forecast is only as good as the actions that follow. Therefore, the process should include the people who are responsible for the center's objectives and can create the changes in tactics necessary to stay on plan. Like the budget itself, the forecast may involve all members of the shopping center team.

Redevelopment

When a shopping center faces redevelopment, the business plan process becomes a little more complex. The complexity arises from both the investment return objectives of ownership and the need to predict a longer future period.

There are several reasons to consider redevelopment. Arguably, the best reason is to meet new and increasing consumer demand. If the market has grown and demographics have improved, an opportunity could present itself to add department store(s) and/or gross leasable area. Sometimes the same market phenomena could require a defensive strategy if new competition is entering the marketplace or if existing competition is expanding.

Additional competition might also compel center management to consider remodeling the property to update its look or add amenities. When redevelopment is a defensive strategy, adding new department stores or tenant area may not always be part of the plan. Remodeling or a face-lift is often harder to sell to ownership, because it may be difficult to demonstrate a return on investment. The only argument might be the threat of value erosion, and that is often difficult to prove.

PRO FORMAS

A pro forma is the developer's estimates of all costs of planning, developing, building, and operating the center or an expansion. From estimates of revenue and expense, the developer computes anticipated net income and the projected value.

If the business plan includes redevelopment, a pro forma will probably be required. Most budget teams will find it easy to explain why the shopping center needs redevelopment. It is sometimes more difficult to explain to ownership why it should invest additional money in the center for the redevelopment. That is the job of the pro forma—to furnish the information about the investment and the financial returns to ownership.

The pro forma begins with an assessment of market demand. Current demographics serve as the basis, but what is really important are growth projections. Population inflow, housing starts, highway construction, business expansion, job growth, and major infrastructure projects all are evidence of growth. An expanding competitive environment may also demonstrate growth.

The total investment in a redevelopment will include both hard and soft costs. *Hard costs* refer to the brick-and-mortar elements of land, building, and building improvements. *Soft costs* include architectural fees, interest on loans, payroll, and indirect expenses. The pro forma will include all hard and soft costs incurred throughout the duration of the redevelopment project.

The developer will often attempt to abate some costs by securing participation from the local municipality. This participation may come in the form of a bond issue in which the development is awarded the benefit of the proceeds and the bonds are paid back through increased sales tax revenues. The municipality might also grant a reduction of real estate taxes for some period. Either way, the pro forma must take into account the potential reduction in cost.

SALES PROJECTIONS

Revenue projections must begin with sales projections. A redevelopment or center expansion must usually capture additional market share to be economically viable. Current market share can be calculated by dividing total center sales, including anchors and outparcels, by projected GAFO (General merchandise, Apparel, Furniture and home furnishings, and Other shopper goods) sales.

Total household income for a trade area is the result of multiplying the total number of households in the trade area by the average income. This is also the potential for GAFO sales. In the United States, GAFO sales currently average between 12 and 13 percent of total household income. So you can project GAFO sales for a trade area by using that average.

To estimate future sales for the center, the developer predicts how much the center's share will increase. If the redevelopment includes the addition of an anchor, the incremental change in market share will probably be greater than if it does not. The developer will use market research specialists to form the assumptions for growth. The projection will also include an estimate of non-GAFO store sales and sales produced by shoppers outside the trade area.

Here's a template for this analysis:

Total households	________________
Average income	($) ____________
Total household income	($) (line 1 × line 2)
Estimated GAFO potential	× 12%
Projected GAFO sales	($) (line 3 × line 4)
Center's market share	share percentage
Center's GAFO sales	($) (line 5 × line 6)
Plus non-GAFO store sales	($)
Projected sales from trade area	($) (line 7 + line 8)
Plus sales from outside trade area	($)
Total projected center sales	($) (line 9 + line 10)

RENT PROJECTIONS

Once total sales potential is known, potential rent revenue can be determined. Pro formas can be complex in the number of variables that must be addressed. For purposes of this discussion, the pro forma process described will be fairly basic in order to demonstrate some of the principles.

For this example, take a center where total projected center sales are $190 million and the three existing anchor stores do $75 million annually. The redevelopment includes a fourth anchor with projected annual sales of $25 million. Potential sales for the center's small shops are the difference between total projected center sales and estimated anchor sales, or $90 million.

Assume that the center is 300,000 square feet and is 85 percent occupied. Nonsales reporting tenants occupy 10,000 square feet. Annual sales volume for the small-shop tenants is $70 million. The estimate of unrealized sales potential is the difference between small-shop potential of $90 million and current sales, or $20 million, as summarized below:

Total projected center sales	$190,000,000
Less: existing anchor sales volume	75,000,000
Less: proposed fourth anchor estimated sales volume	25,000,000
Potential small-shop sales	$ 90,000,000
Less: existing small-shop sales volume	70,000,000
Unrealized small-shop sales potential	$ 20,000,000

The redevelopment includes an assumption that the existing center's occupancy will stabilize at 90 percent. That 5% increase in occupancy, an additional 15,000 square feet of small shops, is expected to produce $4.5 million in sales. This still leaves $15.5 million in unrealized sales potential.

Unrealized small-shop sales potential	$20,000,000
300,000 square feet GLA	
×0.90 stabilized occupancy rate	
270,000 square feet stabilized occupied area	
255,000 square feet current occupied area (85%)	
15,000 sq. ft. increased occupancy in existing center	
Estimated sales for increased occupancy in existing center at $300 per square foot	4,500,000
Unrealized small-shop sales potential	$15,500,000

The redevelopment also includes a 50,000-square-foot expansion of additional small-shop space. By absorbing the $15.5 million in unrealized sales potential, that expansion is projected to produce $310 per square foot.

Unrealized small-shop sales potential	$15,500,000	
Divided by expansion area	50,000	sq. ft.
Sales per sq. ft. potential for expansion area	$ 310	per sq. ft.

Now that the developer has estimated the sales productivity of the center, he or she can estimate rent. In this example, the developer is using the 8 percent rent-to-sales ratio of the existing shopping center. Therefore, the pro forma assumes an average rent for the expansion at approximately $25 per square foot.

Sales per sq. ft. potential for expansion area	$310 per sq. ft.
× 8% rent-to-sales ratio	×.08
Pro forma rent for expansion area	$ 25 per sq. ft.

To recap, in order to forecast rent in any pro forma, the developer must know:

- The sales potential of the trade area
- Estimated sales for anchor stores
- The sales produced by existing small-shop tenants
- The proposed area of the development or the expansion.

This process can work in a different order even though all of the data elements are the same. For instance, the developer might know that he or she must get rent of $25 per square foot but does not know how much gross leasable area has to be built to achieve that goal. Using this example, the developer could divide the $15.5 million in unrealized sales potential by the $25 targeted rent. That result would be multiplied by the 8 percent rent-to-sales ratio to determine that 49,600 square feet would have to be built.

LEASING ASSUMPTIONS AND INCOME PROJECTIONS

A redevelopment pro forma's leasing assumptions include the rental rates and occupancy for any expansion, as well as any increase or improvement expected in the existing space. The example given, you will recall, included sales volumes from the incremental 5 percent occupancy realized in the existing shopping center.

The leasing assumptions must include realistic expectations for tenant opening dates as well as rents. Pro forma leasing assumptions must also include some consideration for recoveries. A developer may very well use recovery ratios to estimate revenue from CAM and other add-on charges.

Whether the redevelopment is an expansion or a remodeling, there may be increases in expense resulting from the change. If redevelopment includes a theater addition, for example, public safety coverage may be adjusted due to later operating hours. When a remodeling includes a change in floor covering, janitorial expense may change too. The pro forma must address the recovery of any incremental expense arising from the redevelopment.

For example, assume that recoveries are 100 percent. This is to keep the example basic and focus on income. Assume that under the leasing assumptions for the 50,000-square-foot expansion, occupancy is projected to stabilize at 90 percent. You already know that you are adding 5 percent occupancy to the existing center. At average rental rates of $25 per square foot and recovery of 100 percent, the redevelopment is producing $1,125,000 net income in the expansion and adding $375,000 to the existing center. The total net income for the redevelopment is $1.5 million, as summarized below:

Expansion area	50,000 sq. ft.
×90% stabilized occupancy	×0.90
Stabilized occupancy expansion area	45,000 sq. ft.
× pro forma rent	× $25 per sq. ft.
Net income* for expansion area	$1,125,000
Increased occupany in existing center	15,000 sq. ft.
× pro forma rent	× $25 per sq. ft.
Net income* for increased occupied area in the existing center	$375,000
Plus: net income* for expansion area	1,125,000
Total net income* for redevelopment	$1,500,000

*Assuming 100% recovery of expenses

RETURN ON INVESTMENT

As stated earlier, a pro forma includes estimates of revenue, expense, and cost. In the example given, assume the existing shopping center's parking is adequate to support the new anchor store and the 50,000-square-foot expansion. This is unrealistic, but it helps to keep the example basic. So there are no costs for parking. The building addition will cost $100 per square foot, or $5 million.

Pro forma costs also include any payments or concessions that the shopping center owner makes to the anchor stores. This may include payments to existing anchors as consideration for their consent to the redevelopment, as well as payments to new anchors. The example will include a $5 million payment to the new anchor. Therefore, total costs for this redevelopment are $10 million. The annual net income produced by the redevelopment is $1.5 million.

The final part of the pro forma will describe the owner's *return on investment,* or *ROI.* Return on investment is that part of an investment's return which is in addition to the return of the investment's capital. In this example, the shopping center owner must be able to get back the $10 million invested for the redevelopment before any return is realized.

In ROI analysis, therefore, some assumptions are made about a property's disposition in order to determine its total value. A typical approach to ROI analysis is to forecast the redevelopment's cash flow for ten years and to assume that the property is sold in the eleventh year. The sale price is generally the capitalized value of the tenth-year cash flow.

The capitalized value is calculated by dividing the cash flow or net operating income by a capitalization rate (cap rate). A cap rate is the ratio of income to price. The market and the quality of the property will determine the cap rate. To select a cap rate for an analysis, an appraiser will look at comparable property sales and their cap rates as well as characteristics of the shopping center. For instance, a shopping center that dominates its trade area may have a better cap rate than a shopping center in an over-retailed market even though everything else about the centers is the same.

The ROI analysis will include a discounted ten-year cash flow and sale price to estimate the value of the property in the current period. A discounted cash flow recognizes the time value of money, or the principle that a dollar in hand today is worth more than one received in the future. The analysis uses a discount rate to convert future income to present value.

Assume that the discounted value of the redevelopment is $11.5 million, so the owner recovers the investment plus $1.5 million. The incremental $1.5 million represents the return, at a rate of 15 percent.

If a 15 percent return achieves the owner's investment goals, the pro forma would be complete. What if, however, the owner's hurdle rate was 20 percent? This owner will not invest additional money in the shopping center unless he or she could realize an increment of $2 million.

That is when the developer would go back to the ROI analysis and ensure that all of the upside generated by the redevelopment had been recognized. For instance, could overall center sales be expected to increase at a higher rate over the next few years as a result of the redevelopment? If so, would those increased sales make higher rents possible for tenants renewing in the existing center? Would the redevelopment improve the outlook for remerchandising the center? Would higher sales and rents improve not only the cash flows for the next ten years but the cap rate as well?

Since the example given has been very basic, it is important to recognize that the impact of a redevelopment on a shopping center can be complex. The full impact must be measured in the ROI analysis if the developer is to be successful in getting approval from the shopping center's owner.

Summary

Understanding the shopping center owner's investment objectives for the property is perhaps the most essential component of the business plan process. The business plan is management's promise to ownership to produce certain results, and the business plan team must understand ownership's expectations if it is to deliver. If the shopping center has debt and the mortgage specifies requirements for rent and occupancy, the team must know those requirements if it is to meet them.

The team must also know for whom and for what purposes the business plan is prepared. The business plan may serve as the basis for the property's valuation. That has ramifications throughout the plan but particularly for leasing assumptions. The operating budget may be used to project the timing of cash needs for the upcoming year. In that case, a budget prepared using the accrual method of accounting may have to be augmented with a cash-flow projection.

Finally, the business plan is management's road map. The plan and its design should help the team manage the property and do its job well. The team's responsibility is to monitor the plan and make corrections to the course throughout the year in order to meet plan objectives.

Kate M. Sheehy is Vice President at Jones Lang LaSalle, Atlanta, Georgia.

5 | Retail Leasing

John E. Phelan, CLS

In discussions of retail leasing, merchandising considerations and complements to the tenant mix are inevitably the focus of the conversation. Leasing has creative elements that most participants would define as an art rather than a science. Still, large investments made in shopping centers are undertaken because retail real estate is an income-producing asset, and the foremost goal of a leasing representative is to maximize that income by completing financially viable lease transactions with retailers and service tenants. Of course, the cornerstone of maximizing property value is developing an appropriate tenant mix that will appeal to the largest audience in a given marketplace, thus ensuring the highest level of sales productivity that will sustain peak market rents over the long term.

As the industry has grown and matured, the infusion of institutional and public capital has heightened the necessity of increased financial scrutiny from analysts and asset managers. Although real estate is and always has been defined as a long-term investment, the objective of short-term results is increasingly important. While the leasing representative seeks to husband the property and enhance value over the long term, investment managers often require near-term achievements, creating a seeming contradiction in the direction of leasing decisions. Consequently, the role of the leasing professional today is far more complex than that of times past, and the need for an understanding of quantitative financial analysis has never been greater.

After negotiating a deal with a retailer, a leasing professional generally needs to secure approval not only from senior management within the company, but also often from an analyst or asset manager. How the deal complements the strategic vision for the property is obviously an important factor in approval. But how the deal affects the desired financial performance of the center is also of major importance. Throughout the history of the industry, it has consistently been taught that the subjective factors of merchandising and tenant mix were the most important considerations in the leasing effort. Today, everyone must learn to better defend these essential merchandising decisions with quantifiable results and to understand how leasing decisions affect property value and financial performance. Balancing the expectations of both the merchandising and the financial perspectives of the asset is the cornerstone of astute property management.

Role of the Pro Forma

The first step in the prudent financial management of the leasing strategy is the development of the pro forma. Whether as part of a development study, acquisition analysis, or ongoing business plan, a thorough assessment of market rents is essential to the proper management of the asset. Because minimum rents typically produce more than 90 percent of a property's net operating income (NOI), rent is one of the most critical determinants of value. Each proposed leasing transaction requires a comparison to the pro forma. Even relatively small variances will produce an aggravated effect on value. This multiplier effect can best be understood by examining a ratio known as the capitalization (cap) rate.

The relationship between NOI and property value is typically expressed as a percentage called the cap rate. Cap rates are determined by the overall investment market and will change with the cost of capital or the investor's perceptions of risk. The simple mathematical formula for capitalization rate is depicted below:

$$\text{Cap rate} = \frac{\text{Net operating income}}{\text{Value}}$$

To determine the effect on value that a change in income (such as minimum rent) would have, the above formula needs to be inverted to solve for value. The resulting formula is:

$$\text{Value} = \frac{\text{Net operating income}}{\text{Cap rate}}$$

For example, a $50,000 increase in rent will change the value by $500,000 if the cap rate is 10 percent ($500,000 = $50,000/0.10). Remember that a change in the cap rate will affect value inversely. Thus, decreasing the cap rate to 8 percent in the above example would result in a $625,000 increase in value ($50,000/0.08 = $625,000).

Market Rent

Establishing realistic targets for market rents in each space is an essential exercise that must be undertaken for every property or proposed development. In existing properties with a sales history, this process is often easier and more accurate than in new developments. All rents should be viewed as a reasonable, sustainable percentage of sales affording the tenant an opportunity to generate an attractive return. For the purposes of this exercise, the term *rent* should be defined as occupancy costs including minimum rent, common-area maintenance (CAM) charges, real estate taxes, and any tenant contributions to marketing the property.

In a regional shopping center, total occupancy costs as defined above typically range from 10 percent to 15 percent of the center's sales productivity. One might argue that the stated range is relatively wide, and shouldn't the leasing agent simply choose the highest percentage in the range to maximize rents? However, the center's performance is what drives demand and hence the rental burdens that tenants are willing to assume. In more productive centers performing at perhaps $400 per square foot, tenants feel far more comfortable with their sales projections and will pay for that added predictability. In addition, in higher-volume centers, leasehold improvements as a percentage of sales are generally less, and even variable costs such as labor can be more efficiently utilized than in less productive centers. Consequently, not only does the more productive center enjoy higher nominal rents, but also it can command a higher percentage of total occupancy costs. This fact certainly reinforces the ultimate leasing objective of driving sales to their highest levels. The simple example that follows illustrates the rather dramatic effect sales productivity can have on minimum rents:

Shopping Center	X	Y
Sales productivity	$300	$400
Occupancy costs/sales	12%	14%
Gross market rent*	$ 36	$ 56
CAM, taxes, marketing	$ 12	$ 16
Net market rent**	$ 24	$ 40

*Sales productivity multiplied by occupancy costs
**Gross market rent minus CAM, taxes, marketing

In the illustration, lower demand and higher fixed costs as a percentage of sales drive market occupancy costs down. Assuming ancillary charges of 4 percent of sales in both centers, a retailer negotiating a lease for property X would likely accept a 12 percent total occupancy cost. Net rent to the landlord is this instance would be $24 per square foot. Given the efficiency of higher-volume stores, the retailer would agree not only to a higher nominal rent in property Y but also to a higher-percentage occupancy cost. This would yield a far higher net return to the developer, largely explaining the premium placed on high-volume properties.

When determining market rents for the pro forma, a space-by-space analysis is the only judicious approach. Each space in a center has unique characteristics that affect its appeal to tenants, and those characteristics in turn greatly affect the corresponding market rent. Elements that need to be considered include:

- Size of space
- Proximity to anchors
- Proximity to entrances and traffic flow
- Linear footage of storefront
- Configuration of premises
- Proposed use of premises.

When considering market rents for a center, a general idea of the desired tenant mix is necessary. Often the fashion focus or price point orientation of the center will greatly affect market rents. The average store size or uniformity in size ranges will also affect the level of achievable market rents. Therefore, the only fiscally prudent method of estimating potential rent levels is the performance of a space-specific analysis.

Break-Even Rents

Market rents are often inaccurately described as the level of rent necessary to produce a desired return on the investment or to cover development costs. The inaccuracy in this thinking stems from attributing the level of market rents to the unit costs of the project. In practice, sales potential is the only determinant of market rents, and costs have little bearing on sales potential. This is not to say that a rent-sensitivity analysis is useless in determining project feasibility. During the conceptual phase of a development, a break-even rent level must be established and later compared to a market rent estimate based on researched sales potential. In an acquisition analysis, an identical exercise is undertaken to validate the offering price. Obviously, in an established project, historical sales data supplant estimated sales potential. The step-by-step formulas for determining break-even rents are as follows:

$$\text{Development cost} \times (1 - \text{Loan/Value ratio}) = \text{Equity capital}$$
$$\text{Equity capital} \times \text{Hurdle rate} = \text{Equity cash flow}$$
$$\text{Equity cash flow} + \text{Debt service} = \text{Net operating income}$$
$$\text{Net operating income}/(1 - \text{Vacancy reserve}) = \text{Required gross income}$$
$$\text{Required gross income}/\text{Gross leasable area} =$$
$$\text{Break-even rent per square foot.}$$

Please note that the above series of formulas incorporates only the most basic assumptions of a feasibility analysis. Net recoveries of property expenses are assumed to be zero, percentage rent is overlooked as a factor, and the impact of tax considerations is disregarded. Nevertheless, the exercise produces a solid estimate of the amount of minimum rent needed to produce a viable development project or substantiate a property acquisition.

Rental Feasibility Analysis

Once the break-even rent level is established, a comparison to market rent estimates is made. If market rents are projected to be higher than the break-even level, there will be a greater level of comfort in the project overall. In the reverse case, when break-even rents exceed anticipated market rent, the cost of the project or capital structure may need to be reevaluated. The inherent risks of the project may be reevaluated, possibly causing an adjustment in the anticipated internal rate of return (IRR) (see page 95).

Table 5.1 illustrates the use of the break-even rent formula in a rental feasibility analysis. The assumptions used in this example are as follows:

- 15 percent return (IRR) to the equity partner
- 9 percent debt-service constant
- 5 percent reserve for vacancy and credit loss
- 70 percent loan to value ratio.

Perhaps most important, it is assumed that an independent study based on a space-by-space analysis of the actual lease plan has determined a market rent level of $35 per square foot. This figure represents a weighted average of the rent targets for each space in the property and is supported solely by realistic sales projections.

Table 5.1 establishes that a base minimum rent of approximately $32.48 per square foot is necessary at a stabilized occupancy level for the project to achieve the developer's hurdle rate for equity while continuing to service the property's debt. A separate estimate of market rent for the project concludes that a $35.00-per-square-foot level is reasonable and will be supported by sales. The positive spread in market to break-even rents in this example provides a strong contingency against inherent leasing and development risks. If the development is completed on budget and the leasing pro forma is achieved at a $35.00-per-square-foot market, the developer will enjoy returns far higher than initially anticipated. The developer's position will also be compounded by his leveraged position behind the 70 percent financing.

Every leasing strategy must balance the often conflicting goals of improving tenant mix and achieving financial results. The parallel procedures of determining break-even rent and market rent form the

Table 5.1 Break-Even Rent Analysis

Development cost		$100,000,000	
Permanent financing		$70,000,000	70% loan to value
Equity capital		$30,000,000	
Equity cash flow	15%	$4,500,000	$4.5m/$30m (A)
Debt service	9%	$6,300,000	9% interest rate (B)
Required net operating income		$10,000,000	(A + B)
Vacancy reserve	5%		
Required gross income [NOI/(1 − Vacancy reserve)]		$11,368,421	$10.8m/(1 − 0.05)
Gross leasable area	350,000		
Break-even rent		$32.48	$11.36m/350,000 sq. ft.
Market rent		$35.00	

basis of the leasing pro forma. Incorporation of a tenant allowance budget into the pro forma completes the financial blueprint of the property relative to the leasing effort. Each proposed leasing transaction will now be measured against this blueprint to determine how the deal affects the property from a financial perspective.

Lease Value

As mentioned at the beginning of this chapter, the objective of attaining financial results may conflict with the desire to create an appropriate tenant mix. Consequently, a leasing representative must understand how to quantify the differences between lease proposals and be able to evaluate the impact of leasing decisions on the pro forma. One might argue that using the capitalization formula discussed previously would provide a simple method for determining lease value. Unfortunately, this would produce an inaccurate result. The capitalization formula implicitly assumes that a property will eventually be sold and that some consideration, typically referred to as "residual value," will revert to the equity partner. In many shopping center properties, this residual could constitute 50 percent of present value.

A characteristic of any lease is the presence of a definitive expiration date. Thus, by its very definition, a lease possesses no intrinsic value after the term ends. Hence, no residual value exists in any lease. The absence of any residual value in a lease actually simplifies the process of determining its value. In shopping center valuation, income attributed to the final year of the investment is divided by a capitalization rate, often referred to as the "exit cap." The resultant value represents the expected sales proceeds of the center and constitutes a large portion of present value. Because the theoretical sale occurs far in the future, any anticipated proceeds are less predictable than current income, and a lease can therefore be considered less risky in valuation.

The simple financial value of any shopping center lease is the sum of its projected cash flows discounted to present value. Leases typically provide for the payment of rent in fixed installments over the term. Following the adage that a dollar tomorrow is worth less than a dollar today, these rental flows must be discounted to solve for present value. Because prototypical retail leases are net leases providing for the complete pass-through of all property-related expenses, the simplest method for analyzing present value is to apply the stated discount rate to the minimum rent stream. This assumes that the annual rental payments will equate to the net cash flow of the lease. Applying this approach, an analyst would discount all anticipated rents at the minimum acceptable rate of return for this type of investment. The formula used for this purpose is exactly the same as the one an appraiser would employ when estimating the overall value of the shopping center:

$$PV = CF_1/(1+i) + CF_2/(1+i)^2 + CF_3/(1+i)^3 + CF_n/(1+i)^n$$

Here, **CF** is the annual rent, **i** is the discount rate, and **n** is the number of years in the lease. A simple example illustrates how to solve for the present value of a lease, using the following assumptions:

- 1,000-square-foot store.
- Five-year lease term.
- Minimum rent is $40 per square foot for years (indicated by superscript) one through three, and $50 per square foot for years four through five.
- Lease is completely net (tenant pays CAM, taxes, marketing).
- There is no expectation of percentage rent.
- Discount rate for the center is 12 percent.

Using the above formula, you can determine the lease value:

$$(\$40,000/1.12)^1 + (\$40,000/(1.12)^2 + (\$40,000/(1.12)^3 + (\$50,000/(1.12)^4 + \$50,000/(1.12)^5 = \text{Value, or}$$

$$\$35,714 + \$31,887 + \$28,472 + \$31,776 + \$28,371 = \$156,220$$

In other words, $220,000 in rent distributed over a five-year term as outlined above is equal to $156,220 today. Knowing this figure is not very useful by itself, but it can be used as a means of comparison between a proposed lease and the pro forma or to compare the financial impact of mutually exclusive transactions. Further, a thorough understanding of the mechanics of lease valuation is essential when analyzing existing leases that are targeted for buyouts. Leasing strategies for remerchandising often include the buyout and breakup of large spaces that involve large capital investments. A leasing professional will usually be motivated by some merchandising objective to justify a transaction of this type. Asset managers will demand a compelling financial reason to undertake the project, and, as will be explained later, a more complex lease valuation analysis will be instrumental in providing these assurances.

One additional note regarding the lease valuation formula should be explained. An argument can be made that using the overall discount rate for the property is inappropriate, because an individual lease bears less certainty and potentially more credit risk than the center as a whole. This premise is quite valid, and often a higher discount rate is employed to compensate for any additional risk. At this point, a more in-depth understanding of discount rates is warranted.

Discount Rate

Because the discount rate is defined as the rate that measures return on investment, the choice of discount rate is crucial in determining lease value. Minor adjustments in the selected rate can result in dramatic shifts in the perception of present value. In addition, as the lease term lengthens, the discrepancies in value are subject to greater variations. Therefore, it is essential to a reasonable financial evaluation that an appropriate discount rate is selected. As most shopping centers are appraised either externally or internally on a frequent basis, usually the most prudent discount rate to employ is the one used for the property as a whole.

At this time, a more thorough examination of the components of the discount rate is required. A discount rate is based on the assumption that investors must seek compensation for bearing risk, sacrificing liquidity, and forgoing the current use of capital. In addition, the existence of inflation, which reduces purchasing power, must be factored into the discount rate. Consequently, the discount rate may be simply defined as a summation of the compensation rates for all these aforementioned factors. A significant portion of this compensation is readily priced in the form of Treasury instrument yields. Given the zero risk of default inherent in U.S. Treasury issues, all investments are compared to this risk-free or safe rate of return. The risk-free rate includes both an inflation premium and compensation to the investor for loss of the use of capital.

As real estate investments are typically long term and analyzed under the assumption of a ten-year holding period, you can correlate the safe rate to like-maturity Treasury issues. For example, a shopping center's discount rate would be compared to a ten-year Treasury note. The difference between the two rates is referred to as the *risk premium*. This factor compensates the investor for inherent market risks, business risks, portfolio management, and loss of liquidity. This component is often referred to as the *marginal cost of capital*. In a shopping center, the marginal cost of capital is fundamentally a weighted average that equates the differing risks associated with each individual lease. Other factors affecting the risk premium include competition, future prospects of the business, and the liquidity of the investment.

To illustrate the components of a discount rate, assume that a shopping center is valued using a discount rate of 11.5 percent. If the prevailing ten-year Treasury note yields 5.5 percent, that safe rate might imply a 3.5 percent inflation premium and a 2 percent real return. Subtracting those factors from the nominal discount rate leaves a 6 percent risk premium (11.5 percent discount rate − 5.5

percent Treasury yield) as the *hurdle rate,* or minimum acceptable rate of return, that would be available for other investments with the same degree of risk. It should be noted that the shopping center industry competes for capital not only with other classes of investment real estate, but with the entire spectrum of financial investments (stocks, bonds, money market funds, and so on).

Internal Rate of Return

The term *internal rate of return (IRR)* is often used interchangeably with discount rate. In fact, the IRR is simply a subset of the discount rate. Discount rates and present value have been shown to exhibit an inverse relationship. As the discount rate decreases, the corresponding present value increases and eventually creates value in excess of the initial capital investment. At one point, there is a rate at which the present value of projected cash flows exactly equals the initial investment. This point is the IRR, and the corresponding formula for this rate is:

$$0 = {}_1\Sigma^n[CF_n/(1 + i)^n] - PV$$

Here, **n** is the years in the holding period, **CF** is the corresponding net operating income, and **PV** is the property value or development cost. In this equation, you are solving for **i,** the IRR, and employing a trial-and-error method using successive increments in the rate. As a practical use, if a project produces an IRR that equals or exceeds the investor's hurdle rate, that project would warrant further investigation. Projects falling short of that hurdle rate would require a reexamination of the assumptions or a repricing.

Comparative Lease Analysis

As discussed earlier in the section on lease value, it was stated that applying the lease valuation formula to a single lease yields the financial value of the lease but delivers little insight to the merits of the transaction unless used as a basis for comparison. Most often the economics of the lease would be contrasted to some baseline, perhaps the pro forma or budget target for the space. Many times a leasing professional is faced with mutually exclusive options, such as two tenants vying for the same space, and needs to quantify the economic differences in the deals. These types of problems are solved with a *comparative lease analysis.* Table 5.2 quantifies the economic difference between a proposed lease and the development pro forma for the same space:

Table 5.2   Comparative Lease Analysis

		Proposed Deal		Pro Forma	
Size of premises	2,500				
Discount rate	12%				
Rent		Yrs 1–3	$25/Sq. ft.	1–10	$28/Sq. ft.
		Yrs 4–7	$28/Sq. ft.		
		Yrs 8–10	$32/Sq. ft.		

In the above example, the pro forma assumes that the space in question would be leased for a ten-year period at a flat $28.00 per square foot and would generate $700,000 in minimum rent over the term. The proposed deal starts at a lower rate, but actually averages slightly higher, at $28.30 per square feet, and generates more revenue ($707,500) over the life of the lease. A cursory review might create the impression that the proposal has more financial value to the property. Using the appropriate method of comparison, the discounted cash-flow formula, produces a different result. Recall the formula for lease value:

$$PV = CF_1/(1+i) + CF_2/(1+i)^2 + CF_3/(1+i)^3 + CF_n/(1+i)^n$$

Applying this formula to the pro forma, where annual rent ($70,000) is substituted for CF and the assumed discount rate (12 percent) is substituted for i, yields a present value of $395,516. Likewise, replacement of the variables with the specifics of the proposal produces a present value of $388,367, or $7,149 less than pro forma. In other words, proceeding with this lease proposal will reduce the value of the property by $7,149. In practical terms, this difference is insignificant and certainly not a valid reason to reject the proposal; it merely illustrates the procedure utilized to compare leases. Actually, pursuant to current accounting conventions, the proposed deal would yield a higher accounting value, due to *rent leveling.* In this purely accounting process, the average rent is deemed income in each year throughout the lease regardless of the actual schedule of payments.

This example displays the procedure for evaluating the effect of a proposed lease on the property's pro forma or budget. As can be seen, this proposal encompasses a "clean" deal without complicating economic terms that can affect the value. Of course, a significant portion of shopping center leases contain economic provisions that differ from the basic one and can substantially change the financial analysis. Generally, complicating factors in a lease transaction fall into two categories:

1. Negotiated inducements that will definitely occur, such as tenant allowances or free rent periods.
2. Events that are contingent upon unknown factors, such as common-area caps or offsets and termination options.

While the discounted cash-flow analysis for lease valuation is utilized in each case, there is one major difference in procedure. Negotiated inducements to a lease are quantifiable and can be timed accurately. Therefore, the valuation process can anticipate these events and account for them rather easily. In the second case, there exists no absolute certainty that the provision will ever be activated; consequently, the valuation must assign a "certainty equivalent" to the event and estimate its effect on value. Obviously, should any severe remedy provision actually be invoked, the ultimate economic value of that lease will be far different from its original expectations. For instance, if a tenant exercises a termination right in the fifth year of a ten-year lease, the actual benefits of that lease to the landlord will certainly be far less than what was anticipated when the lease was first executed. Still, a financial analyst must have some method of reasonably evaluating the merits of a lease with this type of provision. Both categories of complications will be discussed in the ensuing paragraphs.

Negotiated Inducements

A *negotiated inducement* can be defined as any incentive offered by the landlord to persuade the tenant to commit to a lease. Perhaps the most common example is the payment of a tenant construction allowance. The distinguishing characteristic of a negotiated inducement is that it is quantifiable in both the amount and the timing of the payment. There are two equally valid methods of accounting for the payment of a tenant allowance in lease valuation. The simplest method is to deduct the entire amount of the tenant allowance from the net present value (NPV) of the lease. For instance, in the comparative lease analysis example above, the value of the proposed lease was found to be $388,367. If the landlord agreed to a $50,000 tenant allowance in this transaction, an analyst might simply subtract the allowance from the value of the lease to arrive at an adjusted lease value of $338,367. This method is valid only because a tenant allowance is typically paid in the beginning of the term, and one therefore need not attribute a return to compensate for the additional capital investment of an allowance.

The second method entails figuring the appropriate effective rent, as opposed to the nominal rental rate. This method provides a quick manner of comparison to the pro forma that is almost always expressed in terms of rent per square foot. One of the most prevalent mistakes made by leasing professionals when figuring effective rents is to amortize the tenant allowance on a straight-line basis over the term. Again referring to the example used in comparative lease analysis, the average nominal rental rate over the ten-year term was said to be $28.30 per square foot. Providing a $50,000 allowance payable at lease commencement would certainly affect the effective rent of the lease. Incorrectly applying a straight-line amortization of the inducement would yield an effective rent of $26.30 per square foot ($28.30 − [$50,000 allowance/2,500 sq. ft./10 years] = $26.30). This result fails to provide a return to the landlord for the additional capital investment.

The proper method of resolving this problem involves figuring a constant that will fully amortize the allowance over the term of the lease, including a compensatory return to the landlord. The calculation involved is exactly the same as a lender would employ to figure a home mortgage payment. To amortize a $50,000 allowance over a ten-year term at the assumed discount rate of 12 percent, a tenant would be required to pay $8,849.21 per year or $3.54 per square foot. Thus, the real average effective rent of this proposed lease would be $24.76 per square foot. In other words, this proposed lease with a $28.30-per-square-foot nominal average rent and a $50,000 ($20.00

per square foot) allowance equals a deal with a $24.76-per-square-foot average rent and no allowance.

All other negotiated inducements to a lease are handled in a similar manner. Simply deduct all consideration or landlord payments from the cash flow (in the case of a lease, cash flow would be the rental payments) in the year paid and use the discounted cash-flow formula to arrive at the lease value. Conversely, one could deduct the amortization constant from cash flow in each year of the lease to solve for effective rent.

Probabilistic Risk

Accounting for events that would affect lease value, but are not a certainty, presents a far more complex problem in financial analysis. An analyst must assess the additional risk inherent in a lease containing negative provisions that may or may never be invoked. This is accomplished by assigning a probability factor to the trigger event and subsequently adjusting cash flows based on this probability. One major difference in this approach is that, because the analyst has already accounted for the elements of risk, the discount rate used might be adjusted downward to more appropriately reflect the risk of the transaction.

In a shopping center lease, sometimes a tenant is provided with a termination right occurring during the term that is perhaps based on some objective criteria such as sales performance. A termination right is obviously a severe penalty for the landlord and would dramatically affect the overall return on that particular lease. At the time the transaction is proposed, the risk of termination needs to be estimated and expressed quantitatively. To begin this process, the analyst must assign a probability factor to all potential outcomes in the transaction. The result of this exercise will be an array composed of all potential outcomes and their associated probabilities. This array is referred to as a *probability distribution.*

Probability may be defined as the degree of certainty associated with any potential outcome. A single potential outcome must have a range of probability from zero to one. If there is no possibility that a potential event will occur, the probability factor will be zero. On the other hand, a probability of one indicates certainty that the event will occur. Because each event is mutually exclusive and something *must* occur, the sum of all values in the probability distribution must equal one.

After assigning probabilities to all potential outcomes, a unique set of cash flows is projected for each outcome. Each set of cash flows would then be discounted back to present value and multiplied by the corresponding probability factor. The summation of these present values would represent the expected value of the lease. Obviously, this method has some severe shortcomings, because the assigned probabilities must be estimated and have a great potential variance. Table 5.3 demonstrates the use of probability to evaluate the additional risk associated with the inclusion of a termination right. The assumptions used will be the same as in the comparative lease analysis, except that the tenant would have a sales performance clause permitting termination of the lease upon notice at the end of the fifth lease year.

Table 5.3 Proposed Deal

Size of premises	2,500		
Discount rate	12%		
Rent		Yrs 1–3	$25/Sq. ft.
		Yrs 4–7	$28/Sq. ft.
		Yrs 8–10	$32/Sq. ft.

Termination by tenant after year 5 based on sales threshold of $500,000

To determine how the presence of this termination clause affects the value of the lease, the analyst must first evaluate the likelihood that the tenant will fail to achieve the minimum sales threshold. A careful review of the tenant's average store sales and productivity relative to comparable tenants with known sales is necessary for this purpose. Assume that a prudent assessment of sales potential results in a 25 percent chance that the termination provision will become active. Another outcome in this transaction is that the lease will remain in full force and effect for the entire term. Another possibility could be that the tenant falls short of the performance criteria, but remains in place and renegotiates the economic obligations for the remaining term. But for the purposes of this discussion, only the first two options will be explored. By definition, the sum of outcomes in a probability distribution must equal one; therefore, the nontermination option must have a probability of 75 percent.

Using the discounted cash-flow formula, the evaluator would appraise each scenario as if its associated probability was certain. From the previous evaluation of the base lease, it was determined that the deal had a present value of $388,367 for the full term. Assuming the termination will certainly be invoked, the value of the lease would decline to the following:

$$62{,}500/(1.12) + 62{,}500/(1.12)^2 + 62{,}500/(1.12)^3 + 70{,}000/(1.12)^4 + 70{,}000/(1.12)^5 = \$234{,}321$$

The final step in this lease valuation is to multiply the derived present value for each case by its respective probability factor and then to sum the results:

$$(\$388{,}367 \times .75) + (\$234{,}321 \times .25) = \$349{,}855$$

A practical application of this exercise might be to determine an appropriate termination payment as an inducement for the landlord to extend such a termination right. In this example, the difference in present value between the base case and the proposal with termination option is $38,511. It must be remembered that this figure is a present value at the onset of the lease. This figure should be compounded at the discount rate of the property to determine a payment made at the time of termination (the end of the fifth year); under these circumstances, it would grow to $67,870. Some appraisers might argue that the landlord also would experience loss of rental revenue during the period before a new lease commences and that this downtime should be considered in a termination payment. However, interruption in the flow of rent will typically occur when a tenant is replaced and is factored into cash-flow models of the property overall. A termination provision merely accelerates this eventuality.

John E. Phelan, CLS, is the Executive Vice President, Leasing, for New England Development, Newton, Massachusetts.

6

Understanding Rates of Return

Brad M. Hutensky

$\mathbf{P}$resent a deal to most real estate people and their first question inevitably is: *"So what's the return?"*

While the question is innocent enough, answering it invariably leads to a host of other questions, such as:

- Do you mean initial return or over time?
- What discount and capitalization rates should I use?
- Should I allow for the effect of financing and taxes or ignore these factors?

In this chapter you will learn how to answer the question, "So what's the return?" While it will discuss the mechanics of how to calculate rates of return, the real emphasis will be on the far more important skill of *understanding* returns and what they mean.

Specifically, in this chapter, you will learn:

1. How to calculate a simple rate of return
2. How to understand what makes a "good return"
3. How properties are valued using capitalization (cap) rates
4. The concept of the time value of money
5. How to use future value, present value, net present value, and the internal rate of return (IRR)
6. The basics of real estate finance: debt and equity

7. How to develop a "feel" for numbers even if you are not a "numbers person."

Calculating a Simple Rate of Return

There is one simple formula that is critical to understanding how to calculate a simple rate of return (see box).

The relationship return = income/cost is the whole essence of this discussion of simple rates of return. Understand this formula and you will easily learn to understand cap rates, yields, and other methods of calculating return and value.

Remember, perhaps, from your high school math classes that this relationship can be converted to other forms to solve for income or cost:

$$\text{Income} = \text{Return} \times \text{Cost}$$

and

$$\text{Cost} = \text{Income/Return}$$

Generally speaking, one is usually given two of the three components of this formula and is looking to solve for the third.

Simple Rate of Return Calculation

$$\text{Return} = \frac{\text{Income}}{\text{Cost}}$$

Return = Rate of return

Income = Income of the investment

Cost = Cost of the investment

This same formula can be used to calculate capitalization rates (see "How Properties are Valued Using Cap Rates" later in this chapter):

$$\text{Return (cap rate)} = \frac{\text{Income (NOI of property)}}{\text{Cost (purchase or sale price)}}$$

This same formula can be used to calculate values or sale prices given a cap rate assumption:

$$\text{Cost (value or selling price)} = \frac{\text{Income (NOI of property)}}{\text{Return (cap rate)}}$$

Given the importance of really understanding this formula and getting comfortable with its use, start by looking at a few real-life examples.

1. How much interest would a bank account paying 5 percent annually earn in one year?
2. What is the initial return of an investor who purchases a shopping center with net operating income (NOI) of $200,000 per year for $2,000,000?

In the first example, what does the 5 percent interest really mean? If you put $100 in the account on January 1, by December 31 the account will earn $5 in interest. While you can calculate this pretty easily, it is useful to note that the formula in the box could have been used to calculate the same thing.

In this case, return is 5 percent, the interest rate, and cost is the $100 cost of investment; you are trying to solve for the income (the amount of interest). Therefore, using the formula return × cost = income, you obtain $5 as the result (0.05 × $100 = $5).

In the second case, you know income (NOI) and cost (purchase price), and are trying to solve for the return (a.k.a. *yield, initial return, or going-in yield*). Using the same return = income/cost formula, you can see that income is equal to $200,000 and cost is equal to $2,000,000; therefore, income/cost is equal to $200,000/$2,000,000, or 10 percent. Thus you would say, "The going-in yield (or initial yield or return) of this investment is 10 percent."

What Makes a Good Rate of Return?

Now that you can calculate simple rates of return, it is time to address the question: *What makes a good rate of return?*

While there are many factors that could go into determining whether a return is attractive, here you will focus on a few of the most common:

1. Risk
2. Amount of management effort
3. Liquidity
4. Cost of capital

5. Quality of income
6. Certainty of cost.

RISK

The most significant determinant in measuring a rate of return is the amount of risk associated with that investment. Generally speaking, investors will require a higher return to compensate for greater risk in an investment.

For example, a bank's certificate of deposit (CD) might offer an interest rate of 5 percent. This investment is backed by the bank's promise to pay the initial investment plus interest at the end of the CD's term. While banks do not usually fail, some have, and so there is a risk involved in this investment, however small.

Not surprisingly, if one invests instead in a U.S. Treasury note, the 4 percent interest rate reflects a lower risk since this investment is backed by the full faith and credit of the U.S. government, which is obviously less risky than even the country's strongest bank. (Note that these rates change over time, but the relationship is generally right.)

If, instead, you decide to invest your money in the stock of a high tech start-up, you may have the opportunity to earn returns of 25 percent or more. However, this investment would certainly be riskier than either the bank CD or the Treasury notes, and the higher yield reflects that risk.

Similarly, in the world of shopping centers, different properties will have different risk profiles based on many factors. For instance, assume you were comparing two shopping centers, one in a declining neighborhood that is losing population annually and the other in a high growth market with an increasing population. You would say that the first property has more "market risk," and, all other things being equal, an investor would require a higher rate of return to invest in that property if given the choice. Now compare two centers with similar income levels. The first shopping center has a national supermarket chain on a long-term lease as its only tenant, and the second has many small, local tenants that experience high tenant turnover. In this case you would say that the second center has higher "income risk" in that there is a higher risk that the income flow will not continue (see "Quality of Income," below).

Table 6.1 shows some important characteristics of a shopping center and how each affects the risk of the property.

Table 6.1   Factors that Affect Risk

	Lower Risk	Higher Risk	Comment
Anchors	Strong sales, modern stores, long-term leases	Weak sales, out-of-date format, limited term remaining	Landlord benefits when anchor is stable at this location
Term	Long term	Short term	Shorter-term leases mean there is a risk the rental stream will stop if tenant does not renew
Credit	Strong—tenant's ability to pay rent *not* dependent on performance in location	Weak—tenant's ability to pay rent dependent on performance in location	Ideally, tenant will be able to sustain slow start-up or down year
Market	Growing population	Declining population	Stable or growing population ensures future sales
Sales	Strong	Weak	Tenants will generally not leave locations where sales are strong

EFFORT

In addition to risk, another consideration in judging a return is the amount of effort needed to generate that return. Is the return passive, requiring little effort on the investor's part? Depositing money in a bank requires nothing more than making the deposit and waiting. Similarly, buying a Treasury note is a purely passive investment. Other investments require more effort on the investor's part. Buying a shopping center and managing and leasing it is an example of a more active investment. In most cases, one would expect a return premium to be given to an investment that requires more active effort on the investor's part. Similarly, passive investments generally provide no effort premium.

Generally speaking, investors will require a higher return to compensate for greater effort on their part in managing an investment.

LIQUIDITY

Another consideration is *liquidity:* how easily can this investment be converted to cash? In general, the more illiquid an investment (that is, the longer it takes to convert that investment to cash), the higher return an investor would require. Investors will require a higher return to compensate for lesser liquidity in an investment.

Real estate is seen as a fairly illiquid investment. Think how long it would take to get back money that you invested in a shopping center. First, someone would have to put together a sales package, locate a buyer, agree on a price, sign a purchase and sale contract, perform due diligence, and close the sale before getting the investor's money back. Compare that to a savings account, which has almost total liquidity: one simply goes to the bank and closes the account. All of the money is returned almost immediately. This explains why a CD, which often allows no withdrawals for a given term and limited liquidity, offers a higher interest rate than a savings account.

COST OF CAPITAL

The *cost of capital* is generally expressed as the interest rate one must pay to borrow the necessary capital to make an investment. In cases where the capital is already available, the cost of capital is the opportunity cost of forgoing other alternative investments with that capital. For instance, if an investor in a shopping center can borrow money at 8 percent, then clearly she would not want to buy a property that offered a return of 6 percent since she would be paying more for her capital than the investment was yielding.

However, if a foreign investor could only find investments in his country that paid 2 percent, then a U.S. shopping center yielding 6 percent could be pretty attractive. The point is, each individual investor's cost of capital will affect whether he or she sees a rate of return as attractive or not.

Investors will require a return on investment that is greater than their own cost of capital.

QUALITY OF INCOME

It is not enough to simply do the mathematics and calculate the return. One must always give considerable attention to understanding the quality of the income and the certainty of the cost (see below). To determine the quality of income, you must look at the quality of the sources of income. Never accept NOI as a given. Always strive to understand the major components of a property's NOI and how reliable they are. The quality of the income reflects the reliability of its components.

Consider the case above of a shopping center that had NOI (income) of $200,000 and a purchase price (cost) of $2,000,000. You will recall that produced a going-in yield (return) of $200,000/$2,000,000 or 10 percent.

Look at the income. What if the $200,000 came from a 25,000-square-foot, publicly traded, high net worth office supply store paying $8 per square foot (PSF) fully net on a ten-year lease ($8 × 25,000 square feet = $200,000). The center contains one credit tenant paying completely net rent with lots of term left.

Now, compare that to a center where the same $200,000 of income is made up of ten 2,000-square-foot local tenants paying $10 PSF on short-term leases ($10 PSF × 2,000 SF × 10 tenants = $200,000). If this center is purchased for the same $2,000,000, the return would also be 10 percent.

Clearly, though, this income stream is not as certain as the stand-alone office-supply store. Many of these small tenants could have financial problems or decide to leave when their leases expire. Few probably have funds to pay rent if sales should take a downturn. The point is, given the choice, most investors would prefer that their income stream came from the more stable source. Investors will require a higher return for investments with lower-quality income.

Similarly, what if, in the above case, one center shows an NOI of $200,000 after subtracting a $10,000 management fee and a $10,000 per year reserve for future capital improvements? If another center's NOI does not make these adjustments, then clearly the quality of the income is not as high.

For example, if both centers were purchased for $2,000,000, both would not yield true 10 percent returns. The second center's true NOI is not $200,000, since after making reasonable adjustments:

Income	$200,000
Management fee	(10,000)
Capital reserve	(10,000)
	$180,000

The real NOI is actually $180,000, not $200,000, since all properties must be managed, and a $10,000 capital reserve is necessary. Thus the revised return:

$$\text{Return} = \frac{\text{Income}}{\text{Cost}}$$

$$\text{Return} = \frac{\$180,000}{\$2,000,000} = 9\%$$

In this case, when you compare the true income of the same property, you see that a $2 million purchase price really produces a going-in return of 9 percent, not 10 percent. A lot of other issues affect the quality of income, such as lease terms and vacant space. See also the discussion of cap rates (below).

CERTAINTY OF COST

Now look at the certainty of cost. The real question is what is the total cost of the investment and how certain you are that it is the cost. When you put money in a savings account, the investment cost is exactly the amount that is invested. When you buy a shopping center, the cost is more than the purchase price; it includes legal fees, closing costs, due diligence expenses, title insurance, and the reserves needed for tenant improvements and other capital repairs. Generally speaking, investors will require a higher return for investments with less certainty in investment cost.

Now consider a leasing deal. What if someone told you rent is $100,000 per year but the cost to prepare the space for the tenant is $500,000. The basic incremental return is 20 percent, you say ($100,000/$500,000 = 20 percent). That seems like a good rate of return. Ignore the source of the $100,000 of income (in other words, does it come from a single credit tenant or a weak group of locals) and focus on the cost of the tenant improvement.

As asset manager, assume your source of information on the cost of the tenant improvement were one of the three below:

Source 1: A clause in the lease that requires a $500,000 payment by landlord to tenant upon tenant's opening.

Source 2: A contractor who has reviewed the tenant's plans and estimated that the work will cost about $450,000; you added a $50,000 contingency.

Source 3: Your in-house leasing agent indicated that the tenant said its build-out should cost about $500,000.

Obviously, the first source indicates a cost that is certain, since it is a specific clause in the lease. There is absolute certainty in the cost component of the return formula.

In the second source, the cost seems like a pretty conservative estimate, assuming the tenant's plans are fairly accurate and the contractor is reputable. While an asset manager can take comfort in the $50,000 contingency, the fact remains that if there is a cost overrun or an unforeseen problem, it is certainly possible that the $500,000 cost estimate could be exceeded.

Now consider Source 3. Obviously, leasing agents are notorious for understating tenant improvement numbers in an effort, conscious or subconscious, to get deals approved. Given its source and the fact that no plans seem to have been prepared yet and no contractor has estimated the work, clearly the cost estimate is suspect. While the work may come in at $500,000, the actual number could be a lot higher.

In short, the asset manager's willingness to accept a 20 percent return will vary on the certainty of cost. While a 20 percent return might be greater for scenario number 1 and possibly number 2, one might have a much higher concern for scenario number 3 because of the great possibility that the actual cost could be higher, which would drive down returns.

How Properties Are Valued Using Cap Rates

The term "cap rate" (or more formally, "capitalization rate") is the main method for valuing income-producing property. In very simple terms, a cap rate is nothing more than the return component of the simple return formula (return = income/cost) introduced above.

You will also see that deciding on an appropriate cap rate will depend on all of the factors discussed above in the section "What Makes a Good Rate of Return?" In short, the key thing to remember is that "cap rate" is really only a fancy name for a simple rate of return.

Before you continue, it may be helpful to get a quick overview of real estate appraisal techniques. There are three methods for valuation:

1. *Sales comparable approach*: comparing the subject property to the selling price of similar properties that have sold recently.
2. *Cost approach*: calculating the replacement cost if the property were reproduced today.
3. *Income capitalization approach*: the property's income is capitalized by an appropriate rate to yield a value.

Generally speaking, residential homes use the sales comparable approach and commercial (retail) properties use the income capitalization approach. However, while most buyers of a shopping center would rely on the income approach, investors would also consider how the purchase price compares with both the selling price of other shopping centers in the area and the replacement cost of the shopping center if rebuilt today. The main method for valuing shopping centers is ultimately the cap rate.

CALCULATING CAP RATES

Before discussing how to use cap rates, it is helpful to review the simple return formula from above:

$$\text{Return} = \text{Income/Cost}$$

This is how a cap rate is calculated where the return is the cap rate, income is the NOI of the property, and cost is the purchase price (or selling price) of the property. This formula would be used to determine the property's cap rate based on the known NOI and a particular purchase price.

Note that the same formula can also be rearranged to determine a purchase price or value given the property's NOI and an assumed cap rate:

$$\text{Cost (price)} = \frac{\text{Income (NOI)}}{\text{Return (cap rate)}}$$

Less common, but using exactly the same concept, one could determine what NOI must be present if one knew the property's selling price and selling cap rate:

$$\text{Income (NOI)} = \frac{\text{Return (cap rate)}}{\text{Cost (price)}}$$

In summary, then, a cap rate is little more than an expression of the relationship between a property's NOI and its value (presumably its price).

DETERMINING THE APPROPRIATE CAP RATE

Choosing a cap rate is merely a way of saying you are choosing the appropriate rate of return that the market would expect if it were buying the property being valued. Most of the factors have been covered in more detail in the discussion above of factors that affect rates of return. However, a few additional issues include:

1. *Cap rates of similar properties*: if a similar shopping center in the market sold for a 9.5 percent cap rate, that may provide an indication of what the subject property might sell for.
2. *Risk*: generally, *the higher the risk* the higher the amount of return an investor would require and *the higher the cap rate.*
3. *Future upside/risk*: if a property has a lot of future upside (say, vacant space that is leasable), a buyer might take a lower rate of return up front with the anticipation of a higher return in the future. Similarly, future risk (an anchor whose lease terminates in two years and may not renew) would require a higher rate of return/higher cap rate.
4. *Quality of income*: probably the most important determinant in calculating the cap rate. The discussion of the quality of income regarding rates of return above is especially applicable for cap rates.
5. *Cost of capital*: as with any rate of return, cap rates will generally rise as interest rates rise and investors will expect higher rates of returns in order to invest in a particular shopping center.

The key concept to remember is that cap rates are not magical formulas or highly technical calculations; cap rates merely express the mathematical relationship between income and price.

The examples that follow provide an opportunity to make sure you understand how to utilize the cap rate (the answers are on page 136 at the end of this chapter):

1. Given an investment with a net operating income of $1,000,000, calculate the value assuming the following cap rates:
   a. 10%
   b. 9%
   c. 8%
   d. 11.7%
2. Indicate the effect the following characteristics would have on the cap rate of a shopping center and explain why:
   a. High risk
   b. Long-term leases with creditworthy tenants
   c. A lot of local tenants; short lease terms
   d. Many layoffs announced by the town's major employer
   e. No management fee or capital reserves included in income numbers
   f. A large tenant's lease expires the next year and the space can easily be leased at a much higher rent.
3. Calculate the going-in cap rate of an investment that yields an NOI of $1,200,000 in year one at the following purchase prices:
   a. $15,000,000
   b. $12,000,000
   c. $10,000,000
   d. $9,750,000
   e. $11,491,842
4. Which of the above purchasers will have the highest return on investment in year one?

The Time Value of Money: Why Time Really Matters

If people were asked what they would prefer, $100 today or $100 one year from now, almost everyone would choose $100 today (unless you were a compulsive shopper who would value someone forcing you to save $100!).

Why would someone prefer the money today? Well, if you get the $100 today, *you* have it today! *You* can spend it, *you* can invest it, or *you* can sleep easy knowing it is stuffed in your mattress.

This example really illustrates the essence of the *time value of money,* which is a concept critical to an understanding of *present value* (PV), *future value* (FV), and *net present value* (NPV), which we will discuss below.

The Time Value of Money simply means that one would prefer a payment today to a payment of the same amount in the future because the payment received today can be used or invested immediately.

At the risk of belaboring the obvious, make sure you agree that time really matters when it comes to money. What if you were asked: Would you rather have $10 or $1 million if you were paid right now?

It is safe to say that most people would choose the $1 million. It is worth more. Now, what if you were made to choose between $10 today or $1 million in 500 years. Most people would choose the $10. Why? Well, 500 years is a really long time! Since neither they nor their children nor even their great-grandchildren are likely to be around in 500 years, what are the chances that one of their descendants will be around to receive it? Highly remote. But the $10 is still $10, so that is at least worth $10 in groceries today.

One more question. What if you were given the choice between $10 today or $1 million in 100 years, what would you choose? This choice might be a little harder. Why? First, depending on your age and the future of medicine, it is unlikely, but possible, that you might be around in 100 years; certainly it is likely that your children or grandchildren will be around to enjoy the $1 million. Second, it is more likely that the person making the offer, or one of his or her descendants, will be alive to pay the $1 million in 100 years than 500 years. It may make sense to forgo $10 today if your descendants could get $1 million in the future.

In fact, assuming you knew some source that would invest money at the rate of 13 percent per year, it would be possible to choose the $10 option, spend $5 immediately and invest the other $5. Assuming you received at least 13 percent return per year, you could still leave a bank account that would be worth more than $1 million in 100 years to your descendants.

So, how one answers any of these questions has a lot to do with how he or she equates time and money. In the remainder of this section, you will discover how you can use simple mathematics to help make such investment decisions so that they are not left to guesswork or feelings.

FUTURE VALUE

Future value is the easiest concept to understand, since it relates very nicely to the idea of putting money into a bank account. Assume you put $100 into a bank account that paid interest of 2 percent per year. At the end of one year, the deposit would have earned $2 in interest and the balance of the account would be $102.

If you assume that your only investment choice was to put your $100 in that account or keep it as cash, then it is fair to say that you would view the future value of $100 in one year as $102 ($100 × 1.02).

What if you put your $100 in the same bank account for two years? At the end of two years the bank account's balance would be $104.04 (the .04 represents the 2 percent interest on the $2 earned in the first year ($100 × 1.02 × 1.02). In this case, you would say the future value of $100 today in two years is $104.04.

The chart below lays out the future value of $100 growing at 2 per cent per annum.

Year 0	Year 1	Year 2	Year 3	Year 4
$100.00	$102.00	$104.04	$106.12	$108.24

Note that you have assumed a 2 percent reinvestment rate on your money. The *reinvestment rate* is simply the rate at which your investment will grow each year. Now, what if you assume you can reinvest your money at 4 percent? At the end of the first year your bank account would have a balance of $104 ($100 × 1.04). Table 6.2 shows the future value of $100 in various years at various reinvestment rates.

Table 6.2   Future Value of $100 (Various Rates)

Reinvestment Rate	Year 0	Year 1	Year 2	Year 3	Year 4
2%	$100.00	$102.00	$104.04	$106.12	$108.24
4%	$100.00	$104.00	$108.16	$112.49	$116.99
6%	$100.00	$106.00	$112.36	$119.10	$126.25
8%	$100.00	$108.00	$116.64	$125.97	$136.05
10%	$100.00	$110.00	$121.00	$133.10	$146.41

Mathematically, the future value is generally expressed by the formula:

$$FV = I \times (1 + R)^N$$

where:

   I = the initial investment
   R = the reinvestment rate
   N = the number of years of future value being calculated

A word of warning: PLEASE DO NOT MEMORIZE THIS FORMULA! It will only confuse you. It is a lot easier to simply do the math yourself (i.e., $100 × 1.02 × 10.2 . . .$); then you will really understand what you are doing.

Now, look at Table 6.2 again. You can see that the greater the reinvestment rate, the greater the future value of a given investment. Take two investors who are both looking to invest $100. The investor with a 2 percent reinvestment rate would see this money having a value of $108.24 in four years. The investor with an 8 percent reinvestment rate, however, would see a future value of $136.05 in four years. Obviously, the value these investors place on $100 today is very different because of what they believe they will be able to do with this $100.

At this point it is important to understand two concepts:

1. Time matters
2. Different investors view time differently

PRESENT VALUE

Although present value is merely the reverse of future value, it is usually much harder to understand as a concept. The first thing to remember is the question, "Would you rather have $100 today or one year from now?" Clearly, $100 in the future is worth less than $100 today. In fact, most people would accept some amount less than $100 today to forgo the future $100 payment. The amount you would accept today is in fact your present value of the future $100 payment.

If you go back to the $100 investment, invested at 2 percent, which was discussed above, you will see that the investor's bank balance at the end of the year is $102. You recall that the future value in one year of a $100 reinvested at 2 percent is $102. If you work backward, you could say that the present value of $102 in one year that is discounted at 2 percent, is $100 today.

While the future value calculation uses the reinvestment rate as the rate by which an investment grows to the future, the present value calculation uses the term *discount rate* to name the rate by which a future amount is brought back (discounted) into the present. Both rates, discount rate and reinvestment rate, are rates the investor expects to receive on his or her investment.

First, look at the math. Recall that when you calculated a future value, you multiplied the initial investment amount by the reinvestment rate (i.e., $100 × 1.02). To calculate the present value of an amount in the future, you *divide by the discount rate* (in other words, $102/1.02 = $100).

Table 6.3 shows the present value of $102 in future years when discounted at 2 percent.

Table 6.3   Present Value of $102 Discounted at 2 Percent

PV	Year 1	Year 2	Year 3	Year 4
$100.00	$102.00			
$98.04	$100.00	$102.00		
$96.12	$98.04	$100.00	$102.00	
$94.23	$96.12	$98.04	$100.00	$102.00

Note that the one-year-out scenario is what was discussed above (the exact reverse of the future value example, which showed $100 growing by 2 percent for one year). In short, the present value of $102 one year in the future and discounted at 2 percent is $100.

The next line shows $102 two years in the future; it has a present value of $98.04 today when discounted back at 2 percent. The math here is simple:

$$\frac{\$102}{1.02} = \$100$$

$$\frac{\$100}{1.02} = \$98.04$$

For those who insist on a formula, the following equation can be used to calculate present value:

$$PV = I/(1 + R)^N$$

where:
I = the investment at some point in the future
R = the discount rate
N = the number of years away from the present the investment amount lies

Another word of warning: PLEASE DO NOT MEMORIZE THIS FORMULA! It will only confuse you. It is a lot easier to simply do the math yourself (i.e., $100/{1.02 × 1.02 . . .}); then you will really understand what you are doing.

I would strongly encourage you to calculate the last line of Table 6.3 on your calculator so you are comfortable with the math (i.e., 102/1.02 = 100; 100/1.02 = $98.04, etc.).

It certainly makes sense that $102 one year in the future is worth more today than $102 two years in the future, since the investor is one year closer from being able to use the money. Consistent with this, you can see that the present value of $102 four years in the future is worth even less ($94.23).

Now, what about investors who have different discount rates? Remember that in the discussion of future values, an investor who has a 4 percent reinvestment rate calculated the future value of $100 in one year at $104. Similarly, this same investor would say that the present value of $104 one year in the future is $100 today. But what about $102 one year in the future? That investor would calculate a present value of $98.08 ($102/1.04). Note that the investor with the 2 percent discount rate calculated the present value of $102 in one year at $100.

In short, the 4 percent investor values $102 in one year *less than* the 2 percent investor. This makes sense when you again think of this in terms of future values. The 2 percent investor must have $100 today to put in his or her bank account at 2 percent in order to have a balance of $102 at the end of one year. The 4 percent investor, however, needs only $98.08 in his or her account to grow it to $102 at a rate of 4 percent by the end of a year.

Table 6.4 shows $102 discounted back at various discount rates.

Table 6.4   Present Value of $102 from One to Four Years in the Future

Discount Rate	Years in the Future				
	4	3	2	1	0
2%	$94.23	$96.12	$98.04	$100.00	$102.00
4%	$87,19	$90.68	$94.30	$98.08	$102.00
6%	$80.79	$85.64	$90.78	$96.23	$102.00
8%	$74.97	$80.97	$87.45	$94.44	$102.00
10%	$69.67	$76.63	$84.30	$92.73	$102.00

First, look at the column that calculates the present value of $102 one year in the future: the entries for 2 percent and 4 percent are as discussed above, so look at PV one year out with an 8 percent discount rate (this column can be calculated by dividing 102 by 1 plus the discount rate, i.e., 102/1.08 = 94.44). Note that as the discount rate increases, the present value decreases. Again, this makes sense if you think in the reverse of a future value exercise: the investor with the highest reinvestment rate will require a lower deposit in his or her bank account to have a balance of $102 at the end of the year.

Next, compare the 2 percent and 4 percent rows as you move the $102 investment more years into the future. You can see that the present value calculation diverges even more.

If you compare the present value calculation by a 2 percent investor of $102 four years in the future with an investor with a 10 percent discount rate, you see a wide disparity ($94.23 and $69.67, respectively). In short, this means that the 10 percent investor values $102 in four years as worth less than $70 while the 2 percent investor believes this same $102 is worth $24 more today. This means that if both investors participated in an auction for something both valued at $102 that would be available in four years, the 10 percent investor would bid up to $69.67 while the 2 percent investor would be prepared to bid as high as $94.23 (though with the knowledge that his or her competitor would only bid $69.67).

CHOICE REVISITED: $10 TODAY OR $1 MILLION IN 100 YEARS

Now revisit the earlier question about choosing between $10 today and $1 million in 100 years. Obviously, what makes the question difficult is the fact that the $10 and the $1 million are in different time periods. However, armed with your understanding of present values and future values, you can throw out your "gut feel" analysis and actually calculate an answer.

Using a future value analysis, you could grow the $10 to determine the future value of $10 in 100 years. Assuming you chose a reinvestment rate of 10 percent, you could in fact multiply $10 by 1.1 and then multiply the result by 1.1 and so on 100 times. Armed with a computer or calculator, you would see more quickly that at 10 percent, the future value of $10 in 100 years is $137,806. Table 6.5 shows the future value of $10 in 100 years at various reinvestment rates.

Table 6.5   Future Value of $10 in 100 Years (Various Rates)

Reinvestment Rate	Future Value of $10 in 100 Years
2%	$72
5%	$1,315
10%	$137,806
12%	$835,227
12.2%	$1,000,000
15%	$11,743,135

In terms of the question then, what does this table mean? First, the numbers in the right-hand column are important only in their relationship to $1 million. Remember you are assuming that an investor either takes the $10 today and invests it or elects to receive a $1 million payment in 100 years. The chart above indicates that an investor whose reinvestment rate is 2 percent would choose the $1 million in the future, since reinvesting the $10 at 2 percent would be worth only $72 in 100 years. The 15 percent investor, however, would rather have $10 today and reinvest it, which will produce a "bank account" of nearly $12 million in 100 years. Note that an investor with a reinvestment rate of 12.2 percent would be indifferent about the choice of $10 today or $1 million in 100 years since his or her bank account would be the same in either case.

Alternatively, you could answer the $10 today versus $1 million in 100 years by using the present value analysis to determine how much each investor values in today's dollars a $1 million payment 100 years in the future. What is the present value of $1 million 100 years in the future to an investor with a 10 percent discount rate? Again, you could divide $1 million by 1.1 and then divide the result by 1.1 and continue 98 more times. However, a computer or calculator can quickly calculate the present value of $1 million 100 years away at 10 percent as $72.57. In short, the 10 percent investor would view $1 million in 100 years as worth $72.57 today. Therefore, he or she would elect to receive something that is worth $72.57 today (the $1 million in 100 years) instead of $10 today. Note that this is the same decision our future value analysis above provided for the 10 percent investor: to take the $1 million in 100 years.

Table 6.6 shows the present value of $1 million in 100 years for investors with various discount rates.

**Table 6.6   Present Value of $1 Million in 100 Years
(Various Discount Rates)**

Discount Rate	Present Value of $100 Million Payment 100 Years in the Future (rounded)
2%	$138,000,00
5%	$7,604.00
10%	$73.00
12%	$12.00
12.2%	$10.00
15%	$0.85

What does this table mean? Again, the values in the right-hand column are not relevant except in how they compare to $10. Remember, you are calculating the value of $1 million 100 years in the future and comparing that to the alternative of receiving $10 today.

The present value table provides exactly the same answer as the previous analysis in the future value table. The 2 percent investor values $1 million at $138,000 today. In short, the investor would need that amount to forgo the $1 million payment in 100 years. Note that the 5 percent, 10 percent, and 12 percent investors all value $1 million in 100 years as worth more than $10 today. The 15 percent investor values the $1 million in 100 years as less (this shows it worth just 85 cents!), and so would chose to take the $10 today and reinvest it. As before, the investor with a discount rate of 12.2 percent values the $1 million in 100 years to be worth $10 today, which means he or she is indifferent to receiving $10 today and reinvesting it or waiting for the $1 million payout.

NET PRESENT VALUE

The net present value calculation is quite simply a way to perform a present value calculation on multiple payments in different future years and bring all of these amounts into today's dollars. You learned above that if someone asked for the present value of a $500 payment one year in the future and you were using a 10 percent discount rate, it would be easy enough to calculate an answer of $454.55 ($500/1.1 = $454.55). What if someone asked about the value in today's dollars in an investment that paid $500 at the end of the first year, $1,000 at the end of year 2, and $18,500 at the end of the third year? Using the same techniques you can calculate the answer.

This flow of funds would look as follows:

Today	Year 1	Year 2	Year 3
NOI	$500	$1,000	$18,500

You already determined that the present value of $500 in one year is $454.55 at 10 percent. Now, doing a separate calculation for the payment in year 2, you see that the present value for year 2 is $826.45 ($1000/1.1 = $909.09; $909.09/1.1 = $826.45).

Lastly, you calculate the present value of the year 3 payment, which is $13,899.32 ($18,000/1.1 = $16,818.18; $16,818.18/1.1 = $15,289.26; $15,289.26/1.1 = $13,899.32). Now, adding these three present values together to get the present value of all three amounts, you have $454.55 + $826.45 + $13,899.32 = $15,180.32.

This method of calculating the present value of multiple payments made in various years and adding them all together is called the *net present value*. So, the net present value of the three payments above that are made one, two, and three years in the future is $15,180.32.

Now calculate the NPV for the same three payments, assuming a discount rate of 12 percent ($14,412) and again at 14 percent ($13,695). (Methodology is shown in #5 at the end of this chapter.) Note that the greater the discount rate, the smaller the NPV. If you think back to the discussion of present value, this should make perfect sense. You saw that the greater the discount rate, the smaller the present value in the chart discounting back $102. It follows that if you do multiple present value calculations (in this case three) and add them up, the total will be less if you use a higher discount rate than a smaller one. Alternatively, if you think of having to make three payments of $500, $1,000 and $18,500 in the future, it stands to reason that you will need less money in your bank account up front if the account earns interest at 14 percent than at 10 percent.

What does this mean? Generally speaking, the 10 percent investor would be willing to pay as much as $15,180 for this stream, but the 14 percent investor would pay only $13,695 for the same thing. This all relates back to the differing views on the time value of money.

Internal Rate of Return (IRR)

The internal rate of return can best be understood by looking at its mathematical definition:

- The internal rate of return is simply the discount rate such that the net present value of an investment stream is equal to zero.

To illustrate this calculation, return to the three-year cash stream discussed in the section on net present value. Assume one could purchase this investment for $14,000. Is that a good deal? Hopefully you will remember to consider risk, liquidity, effort, the quality of income, and the certainty of cost before writing a check. However, if you put these issues aside for the moment, you may want to calculate the deal's IRR.

While there are calculators and computer programs that can quickly perform this calculation, it will be easier to understand if you calculate by hand. Looking at the cash flow stream below, note that you write the initial investment as a negative value to show that it is different from the three payments in years 1–3, which are cash inflows. The key here is to make sure the sign of each value reflects whether a payment is an inflow or outflow.

	Year 0	Year 1	Year 2	Year 3
Cash flow:	($14,000)	$500	$1,000	$18,500

Table 6.7 Net Present Value

Discount Rate	NPV of All Cash Flows	NPV of Cash Flows			
		Year 0	Year 1	Year 2	Year 3
10.00%	$1,180	(14,000)	455	826	13,899
12.00%	$412	(14,000)	446	797	13,168
14.00%	$(305)	(14,000)	439	769	12,487
13.00%	$47	(14,000)	443	783	12,821
13.10%	$11	(14,000)	442	782	12,787
13.13%	$1	(14,000)	442	781	12,778
13.132%	$0	(14,000)	442	781	12,777

Look at the first three values in Table 6.7. You obtain the net present value at 10 percent, 12 percent, and 14 percent using the same calculations as above, and then subtracting the $14,000 investment. Note that the combined NPV cash flows at a 10 percent discount rate is equal to $1,180, which is the $15,180 NPV for years 1–3 calculated above less the $14,000 initial investment. The same holds for the other two calculations.

Now, note that the NPV at 12 percent is $412, but at 14 percent is ($305). Remember that the IRR is that special discount rate that makes the NPV equal to zero. Therefore you know that the IRR must be somewhere between 12 percent and 14 percent. If you guess 13 percent and do the calculations, you will see that the NPV is $47. This means that the correct discount rate, the IRR, must be somewhere between 13 percent and 14 percent. By trial and error you can eventually find the discount rate, in this case 13.132 percent, that produces a NPV of zero. You would say that the internal rate of return (IRR) of the above investment is 13.132 percent. You could also say that the discount rate where the NPV of this investment is zero is 13.132 percent, but people might look at you funny. In reality, you would be saying *exactly the same thing*.

What does the IRR tell you? Generally speaking, it is used as an indicator of a deal's rate of return. But be careful! Recall the discussion of what makes a good return, above. All of these rules still apply. For instance, compare two deals both sporting 12 percent IRRs. Are the deals the same? Not likely. What if one shopping center provided income from a single high-credit national retailer and the other one produced the same projected income stream from a group of unsteady local operators? In both cases you might calculate a 12 percent IRR, but obviously the quality of the income making up each IRR is very different.

In short, remember that *all deals with a 12 percent IRR are not created equal.* Review all the issues brought up in the section "What Makes a Good Rate of Return." All apply every time your calculate an IRR. If you forget about the underlying assumptions that go into the numbers on which an IRR calculation is based, the IRR will become a dangerous weapon. If you forget about real estate fundamentals, the internal rate of return becomes, as noted investor Sam Zell put it, "the Infernal Rate of Return." Remember this: the IRR is nothing more than a mathematical calculation that very few people in real estate really understand. Hopefully, you now consider yourself in the minority.

Determining an Appropriate Reinvestment Rate and Discount Rate

While there are some very complicated models and theories about how to select the proper reinvestment rate and discount rate for each investor, for your purposes the determination can be made rather simple. The *reinvestment rate,* which is used in a future value calculation, can generally be thought of as the rate by which you could invest capital. If you put your money into a savings account that yields 3 percent, that is your reinvestment rate. If, instead, you invest in real estate deals that average returns of 12 percent, then that is your reinvestment rate. The analysis need not get any more complicated than that.

Simply speaking, you could assume that a discount rate is about equal to the reinvestment rate and capture the spirit of this discussion. Think of the present value calculation as a two-step process. What is the future value of a $100 payment one year in the future? Well, if you had some money today instead, you could reinvest it at the reinvestment rate. Therefore, if you calculate what amount of money you would need to have today, deposit in a bank account (or wherever you put your money to get your reinvestment rate), and grow it to $100 in one year, that amount is the present value to you today of $100 one year in the future.

However, the discount rate really is more than just the reverse of the reinvestment rate. A discount rate should also reflect all of the issues discussed above in looking at choosing a cap rate. For instance it must look at risk: what is the risk that the $100 payment will not be made at the end of the year? Clearly, if the risk is high that it will not be paid, you would value this $100 payment less in today's dollars than if payment was a certainty. In short, greater risk suggests a higher discount rate. Think of it this way: everything that would demand a higher rate of return by the investor (similarly, a higher cap rate) would also suggest a higher discount rate. ***The discount rate is another way of describing rate of return and is affected by risk, liquidity, effort, cost of capital, quality of income, and certainty of cost, much like cap rates and other measures of return.***

An Overview of Real Estate Finance

Real estate finance today has become a complicated world with its own terminology, techniques, and practices that may seem foreign to many real estate professionals. Luckily, when all of this jargon and structure is peeled away, you will find that real estate finance is still based on a few easy-to-understand fundamental concepts. This section will focus on the key concepts of real estate finance that every professional needs to know and understand.

REAL ESTATE FINANCE CONCEPT #1: DEBT AND EQUITY

In any real estate purchase, the buyer will generally pay for the acquisition with some combination of cash and proceeds from a loan. Think of a house purchase: one generally secures a mortgage loan (debt) of about 70 percent to 80 percent of the price and then pays cash (equity) for the balance of the price.

While the sources for the "loan" and "cash" components can be more complicated in a commercial transaction, in essence the same combination of a loan and cash or debt and equity provide the capital needed to pay the purchase price. Consider the example below:

Price of Property	$1,000,000	
Capitalization		
First Mortgage	$700,000	70%
Cash	300,000	30%
Total	$1,000,000	100%

In this case the buyer has a capital structure of 70 percent debt and 30 percent equity. Alternatively, the buyer could have borrowed a greater percentage of the purchase price (if he or she found a willing lender) and contributed less cash:

Capitalization		
First Mortgage	$800,000	80%
Cash	200,000	20%
Total	$1,000,000	100%

Note how this structure has more debt and less equity than the structure above. There are also lenders who will provide even more debt to a transaction. However, in general, a lender who is providing more than about 70 percent of the purchase price is usually considered to be providing some portion of the equity (cash) piece of the funding. This can be understood when one looks at pricing and risk.

REAL ESTATE FINANCE CONCEPT #2: RISK AND RETURN

Real estate finance is based on the same general risk and reward relationship discussed above: the greater the risk, the greater the reward (or return). In a typical real estate mortgage loan, the return to the lender is the interest paid by the borrower. The risk is that the borrower may not pay back the loan as specified in the loan documents. However, the lender also receives a mortgage on the property as security to guarantee repayment. In simple terms, if the borrower does not repay the loan, the lender can take control of the property, sell it, and take its repayment from the proceeds of the property sale. In short, the lender really has two sources of repayment:

1. The borrower
2. Proceeds from a foreclosure sale if the borrower does not pay.

How does this all relate to risk and return? A few examples below will illustrate this concept and show how the higher percentage of debt lent against the purchase price (or property value), the higher the risk to the lender.

Purchase Price	$1,000,000	
Capitalization		
First Mortgage	$700,000	70%
Cash	300,000	30%
Total	$1,000,000	100%

If the borrower defaulted on the loan—that is, stopped paying according to the loan terms—the lender could seize the property and sell it presumably for about the $1,000,000 price that was paid for the property originally. The lender would receive all of its $700,000 loan proceeds back (the balance of the proceeds would generally go to the borrower).

In reality, however, the borrower usually stops paying the loan only when the value of the property declines significantly (perhaps because the project has lost a major tenant or general values have dropped in the market). Assume there is a 20 percent drop in the value of the property to $800,000. Note that even under these circumstances, the lender would still get repaid if the lender is forced to foreclose on and sell the property. Table 6.8 illustrates this point.

Table 6.8   Anticipated Proceeds from Sale after Change in Property Value

Change in Property Value	New Value	Anticipated Proceeds Paid to Lender	Anticipated Proceeds Paid to Borrower (Owner)
Increase 10%	$1,100,000	$700,000	$400,000
No Change	$1,000,000	$700,000	$300,000
Decrease 10%	$900,000	$700,000	$200,000
Decrease 20%	$800,000	$700,000	$100,000
Decrease 30%	$700,000	$700,000	$0
Decrease 40%	$600,000	$600,000	$0
Decrease 50%	$500,000	$500,000	$0
Decrease 60%	$400,000	$400,000	$0

Note that the lender is protected in full in the case of borrower default even if the value of the property drops 30 percent from the original purchase price. Assuming the original purchase price was a fair assessment of value, this gives the lender a significant margin for error in the event that (1) the borrower does not pay back the loan as promised and (2) the lender is forced to sell the property to reclaim its loan proceeds.

From the above you can see that a lender making a loan of 80 percent of the purchase ($800,000 in this example) price has less margin for error than one lending to 70 percent. Both lenders would be able to recoup their loan proceeds in a foreclosure sale of a price as much as 20 percent less than the original purchase price. However, at a reduction in value of 30 percent, the $700,000 proceeds of the sale would not cover the full $800,000 loan made by the 80 percent lender.

It follows, then, that the lender making an 80 percent loan is taking more risk than the lender making the 70 percent loan. Similarly, a lender making a 90 percent loan ($900,000 in this case) would be taking even more risk, since a reduction in value of more than 10 percent would mean the lender could no longer collect all of its investment in a foreclosure sale. The lender will require more return in the form of a higher interest rate on the loan to reflect the greater risk being assumed. Similar to any investor, the lender will require a greater return (interest rate) for higher risk.

REAL ESTATE FINANCE CONCEPT #3: KEY LOAN TERMS

While a lot of financing terms are thrown around in real estate finance, most terms are based on a few basic loan terms summarized in Table 6.9.

Table 6.9   Key Terms of Typical Mortgage Loans

Loan Term	Definition	Comment
Loan amount	Amount to be borrowed	Usually based on % of value
Interest rate	Return to lender	Many variations and forms
Term	Length of loan	Can vary significantly
Amortization	Repayment of principal prior to maturity	Could range from none to significant
Collateral	Security to guarantee loan repayment	Range from property to personal guarantee
Restrictions	Loan covenants on borrower	Often severe; can affect ability to run property

Loan Amount. The loan amount is usually determined by a percentage of the property's value. As has been pointed out above, the greater the loan is as a percentage of the purchase price (assumed to be value), the less cushion the lender has in the case of a foreclosure sale. This is why most lenders will restrict all loans to a percentage of property value, say 70 percent. This gives the lender an appropriate risk for the interest rate of the loan.

In determining an appropriate loan amount for a given project, lenders will determine the project's value, usually confirmed by a property appraisal, and then calculate the loan amount based on the lender's underwriting criteria and the amount of the value the lender is willing to loan.

Lenders will also look at the relationship between the expected debt service and the projected NOI. This relationship is called the *debt coverage ratio* and is expressed as the ratio between NOI and debt service. For instance, a property with NOI of $1,200,000 per year and an annual debt service of $1,000,000 is said to have a debt coverage ratio of 1.2 ($1,200,000/$1,000,000 = 1.2). Since a debt coverage ratio of 1.0 means that NOI exactly equals debt service, there is little margin for error in that any reduction in NOI means there is not enough cash from the property to pay the debt service. Thus, the higher the coverage ratio the higher the margin for error and the greater the chance the loan will be repaid.

Interest Rate. The interest rate is the return required by the lender to make a given loan. Usually, for real estate loans, they are *fixed rate,* which means they are a set rate that does not change over the life of the loan. Some loans are *floating rate,* which means the interest rate is based on some relationship to a benchmark like the prime rate (the preferred lending rate set by U.S. commercial banks) or LIBOR (the London Interbank Offering Rate), both of which can be found in the *Wall Street Journal.*

The interest rate on a loan should be less than the rate of return required for an equity investment. This is because the debt position has the "first position," which means that all cash flow is first given to the lender to satisfy debt service. Similarly, any proceeds from a sale are first used to pay off the debt. As has been discussed above, the lender who makes a loan equal to 70 percent of the purchase price can withstand a 30 percent loss in value without losing any principal if the borrower defaults and the property is sold. In the same case, a 30 percent reduction in property value would wipe out the equity position. Consistent with the discussion above, the debt position has a lower risk than an equity investment and so commands a lower rate of return.

It should also be noted that a loan may include a participation feature which allows the lender to receive a portion of the available cash flow and/or sales proceeds.

Term. While terms vary, most loans are between three and ten years.

Amortization. Amortization is simply the repayment of a portion of the loan before the end of the loan term. Many loans are "interest only," which means that no principal is paid back prior to loan maturity. Some loans are hybrids in that they contain an initial interest-only period and then convert to an amortizing basis.

In general, lenders like amortization since it reduces the amount of loan proceeds outstanding and also reduces the pressure to repay at the end of the loan term. Borrowers do not generally like amortization because it increases the amount of their loan payment.

How does amortization work? Basically, a loan has a steady payment that includes both interest and principal payments. Over time, the amount of the payment that goes to principal increases until the loan is paid off in full.

The following example shows a $100 interest-only loan at 10 percent and a three-year amortization of a $100 loan at 10 percent.

	Year 0	Year 1	Year 2	Year 3
Interest-only loan	($100.00)	$10.00	$10.00	$110.00
Three-year amortizing loan	(100.00)	40.21	40.21	40.21
Interest		10.00	6.98	3.66
Principal		$30.21 +	$33.23 +	$36.55 = $100.00

The above example shows that in year 1, the principal balance is $100, so the interest charge is 10 percent $\times$ 100 = $10. The balance of the $40.21 payment, $30.21, goes to pay down the loan, which has a balance of $69.79. Moving to year 2, the interest payment is $6.98, which is equal to 10 percent $\times$ $69.79. In year 3, we see that the interest payment is $3.66, equal to 10 percent $\times$ $36.55.

Collateral. The *collateral* is generally the backup source of loan repayment if the investor does not repay the loan as specified in the loan documents. Most real estate loans use the property as collateral and secure their loan via a mortgage. Many loans are made *non-recourse* to the borrower, which means that if the loan is not repaid, the lender can only look to a sale of the property as its source of repayment and not to the borrower.

Other loans are made on a *recourse basis,* which means that if there are not enough proceeds from a sale of the property to repay the loan, the borrower is obligated to pay off the difference. A recourse provision is often called a *personal guarantee,* in that the borrower is using his or her personal assets as a secondary means to repay the loan. Obviously, lenders like this provision since it provides a backup source of repayment in case of problems with the loan. For the same reason, borrowers avoid a recourse provision unless it is the only way they can borrow money for a particular project. A personal guarantee means that in the case of a deal failing, not only could the borrower lose the property, he or she could also lose other nonrelated assets to help repay the loan.

In cases where a lender is providing a number of loans on a group of properties, the lender will often require that the properties *cross-collateralize* the loans. This means that if any of the single property loans are in default—that is, the loan terms are not being complied with (generally nonpayment of debt service is the biggest issue)—the lender can look to the income and ultimately the sale of any of the other properties to satisfy the terms of the loan. This provides the lender with less risk, in that there are more ways it can be repaid than if it could only look to the specific property on which the loan is being made.

In loans to more than one borrower, lenders will usually ask that any guarantees be made *jointly and severally,* which is the same concept as cross-collateralization. What this means is that if there are three partners in a property and each is personally guaranteeing repayment of the loan, each partner is ultimately responsible for full repayment of the loan even though they may only own one-third of the property. The lender can look to all of the partners or any one partner (in other words, the one with the most assets) to repay the loan, which gives the lender the best chance for repayment in the event the property or properties cannot be sold for enough to pay off the loan.

Restrictions. There is no end to the number of restrictions a lender might put on a borrower as part of the terms of the loan. In general, most of these restrictions seek to maximize the chances that the lender will be repaid by restricting or requiring certain practices by the borrower. Some of these requirements may seem unusually onerous, and anyone who has actually read a loan document has seen how draconian some of the loan language actually is. Most loan documents are written based on a modern variant of the golden rule: "Those who have the gold make the rules."

Common restrictions in a loan include restrictions on additional borrowing: the lender does not want more debt on the property, which will place more of a burden on the borrower to repay its loan. All loans today require the borrower to state that no hazardous environmental conditions exist at the property and usually require the borrower to take steps to make sure no such conditions will occur in the future. There are pages of provisions about how insurance proceeds would be used in the case of a fire (in other words, to rebuild the center or pay off the loan) and what would happen if the property were condemned by the city or town. Similarly, the loan will usually restrict the amount of management and other fees the borrower can pay out of cash flow, since the lender wants to make sure it gets paid back before the borrower is unduly enriched.

In terms of requirements, the borrower is often required to provide the lender with an annual budget, and the lender may have certain approval rights to review major leases and capital improvement projects. In other cases, the lender will require all property income be sent to a lockbox, which the lender or its agent controls. The borrower is given disbursements from the lockbox as needed for property expenses and debt service. Such an arrangement is thought to provide the lender with better control of cash, though it can also add a layer of administration that makes it more difficult to operate the property. Usually, the borrower is also required to provide monthly operating reports to the lender, since the lender would ideally like to know about a problem in repayment prior to it actually occurring.

A Word on Taxes

While this chapter will not delve into the effect that taxes have on calculating returns, it would be irresponsible not to at least remind the reader that taxes are an important part of most investment analysis.

For example, assume two investors look at a real estate deal that provides $200,000 of NOI for a $1,000,000 investment. In this case the simple return is 20 percent ($200,000/$1,000,000). Now, to consider the effect of taxes, ask each investor at what rate this additional income will be taxed. If Investor 1 says he or she will be taxed at a 20 percent rate and Investor 2 says a 35 percent rate, their after-tax return on the same investment will be different (for this analysis assume that NOI = taxable income, which is not usually the case but will suffice here).

Table 6.10   Effect of Tax Rates on Investor Returns

	Investor 1	Investor 2
Net operating income (assume = taxable)	$200,000	$200,000
Pretax return on $1 million investment	20%	20%
Tax rate	20%	35%
Taxes payable (tax rate × NOI)	$ 40,000	$ 75,000
After-tax income	$160,000	$125,000
After-tax return on $1 million investment	16%	12.5%

In general, it is recommended that you be aware that taxes do matter and perform all return calculations on a pretax basis. If the return looks favorable after doing all of the other qualitative analysis discussed above, see your Chief Financial Officer or accountant to better understand the tax issues involved.

Developing a Feel for Returns

In completing this discussion of rates of returns, it is important to remember a few ground rules:

1. Never get intimidated by numbers.
2. If someone gives you numbers, think about the source.
3. Don't get bogged down in detail; focus on what's important.

NEVER GET INTIMIDATED BY NUMBERS

First, it is necessary to feel the numbers and keep your wits about you. Never get intimidated; think about what you are doing. Analyze the question being asked and decide whether it makes sense before rushing ahead trying to find an answer. Follow this advice and you will save yourself a lot of wasted time answering questions that don't need answering.

IF SOMEONE GIVES YOU NUMBERS, THINK ABOUT THE SOURCE

Any calculation of return is only as good as the assumptions that are made in the process. Always consider the source of any information you collect in building your model.

For instance, if you have ever seen a television news story describing a major drug raid by the police, invariably the newscaster will add, ''The drugs had a *street value of twenty million dollars.*'' Ever wonder *what street* they are talking about? Obviously, the police have provided the newscaster with the value of the drugs.

The point here is to consider the source of any assumption or input you put into your pro forma. Once you adopt the assumption as your own, your return calculation will forever be affected by any prejudices or inaccuracies embedded in the numbers.

DO NOT GET BOGGED DOWN IN DETAIL: FOCUS ON WHAT'S IMPORTANT

This is really critical. People often get carried away with building a model, or a presentation and a format, or providing the details of some unimportant component or assumption that they totally lose track of the real goal of performing the calculation.

Many problems can crop up when you lose a clear head and get caught up with the numbers. Most of the concepts discussed above are fairly simple, but you can sure get into a lot of trouble if you forget that the calculations are merely tools; *you* have to do the thinking.

Answers to Sample Problems

Here are the answers to the sample questions on pages 114 and 123:

1a. $10,000,000 (1,000,000/0.10)
1b. $11,111,111 (1,000,000/0.09)
1c. $12,500,000 (1,000,000/0.08)
1d. $8,547,009 (1,000,000/0.117)

2a. Increases cap rate: investors demand higher return for higher risk.
2b. Reduces cap rate: High-quality income and less risk creates lower return expectation.
2c. Depends on the market. If the leasing market is strong and rents in place are low, this is a great opportunity and would reduce cap rate. Investors accept a lower going-in return because they can increase it later. If the market is weak, the short-term leases are a risk and the cap rate will be higher.
2d. Increases cap rate because of higher market risk; investors will require higher return.
2e. Increases cap rate: NOI is overstated so a higher cap rate is needed to yield the proper (lower) return when the true NOI is used (net of management fee and the reserves).
2f. Reduces cap rate: this is a great opportunity for future upside; investors would take a lower initial return.

3a. 8%   (1,200,000/15,000,000)
3b. 10%   (1,200,000/12,000,000)
3c. 12%   (1,200,000/10,000,000)
3d. 12.3% (1,200,000/9,750,000)
3e. 10.44% (1,200,000/11,491,842)

4.   Investor 3d who shows a 12.3% yield.

5.   NPV @ 12%

	Year 1	Year 2	Year 3
NOI Today	$500	$1,000	$18,500

$500/1.12 =   446.42

$1,000/1.12 = 892.85/1.12 =   + 797.19

$18,000/1.12 = $16,517.85/1.12 = $14,748.08/1.12 =   +$13,167.93

                                               Answer $14,411.55

NPV @ 14%

$500/1.14 =   438.60

$1,000/1.14 = 877.19/1.14 =   769.46

18,500/1.14 = 16,228.07/1.14 = 14,235.15/1.14 =   12,486.97

                                                 Answer   13,695,02.

Brad M. Hutensky is President of The Hutensky Group, Hartford, Connecticut.

7 | Using Numbers to Manage Your Business

Kenneth S. Lamy

As you may know, the measurement of earnings for any asset class is truly the bottom line in business. It is the only way management is able to keep score regarding the contribution of the components of the operating entity. The ability to measure begins with the high-level expectation for good information being supplied by the various sources of data—that is, the staff of the center management office, the corporate headquarters, and the merchant (tenant). This chapter captures the critical nature of quantitative data analysis to assist in the quality decisions to be made each day.

Lease Management and Reporting

Sometimes known as lease administration, this process represents the paper trail of the life of a lease with property management. The lease, as noted earlier in this book, establishes all of the ground rules, both financial and nonfinancial. Within the lease administration department, the lease is administered by one or more staff members. Their duties could include lease preparation, lease analysis, lease summary, billing and collection, settling disputes, tenant relations, review of tenant reimbursement requests, (tenant improvement allowances), pass-through (CAM) items to tenants, sales reports, certificates of insurance, operating expenses/tenant notification, data entry of the new lease and/or terms, maintenance of information on the property management database for that property, calculation of administrative fees, taxes, HVAC, insurance and utilities, and preparation of the various management reports on a weekly or monthly basis. See Exhibits I and II at the end of the chapter as examples.

Minimum Rent

The basic rent that a tenant will pay the landlord each year in twelve equal, consecutive, monthly installments, usually on or before the first day of each month during the term of the lease, is called the minimum rent or base rent. It is normally computed based on an amount of rent per square foot multiplied by the size of the store (square footage).

The rent paid by a tenant is where the value of a shopping center begins. Next would be to identify whether the lease signed is a gross or net lease. In a gross lease, the tenant pays one flat amount and the landlord pays all other expenses of the center, such as taxes, insurance, and repairs and maintenance of the property. With a net lease, the tenant agrees to pay rent plus a share of the other expenses listed above.

The *rent roll* is a summary schedule listing of all spaces in the center. This would include both occupied and vacant. Many data are noted on this schedule, including:

- Tenant name (DBA—Doing Business As)
- Space number
- Category of retail
- Size of store (square feet)
- Rent-fixed minimum (annual)
- Term of lease
- Commencement date
- Expiration date
- Annual breakpoint
- Percentage rent rate(s)
- Others.

The format and level of information should reflect management's need for quick reference and full-disclosure summary data for their day-to-day use and ownership's ability to analyze the terms of each lease.

Several examples shown in Exhibits III, IV, V, and VI provide you with the types of formats you might encounter. All of these charts (Exhibits I through VI) allow the reader to review the financial picture of a property in areas such as tenant roster, lease summary, tenant ledger card, expiration schedule, minimum rent budget, expiration schedule, vacancy reports, scheduled adjustments, and so on.

With valuation of a shopping center being directly tied to the income approach, the rent and ultimately the net operating income (NOI) establish the value of a property. NOI is calculated by taking the difference between the revenue and expenses of the property. Both depreciation and interest expense would be kept out of the amount computed. Therefore, any change in revenue or expenses would directly affect the value of the center.

Using Sales Reports for Percentage Rent Projections and Occupancy Cost Analysis

In order to establish rent structures that are affordable to a merchant (tenant), one needs to understand the relationship between sales volumes and the occupancy costs of a tenant. Each of these items relate to dollars per square foot. As amounts per foot increase, the amount of rent a tenant can pay grows with it. Rent is truly a function of sales.

Percentage rent is the amount of rent paid in addition to the minimum base rent payment of a tenant. It is an annual rental payment based on a percentage of sales in excess of a stated breakpoint for each tenant. Both the percentage rent rate(s) and the breakpoint(s) are defined in the lease. The landlord receives such a payment (overage) only when sales reach a higher volume than they may have achieved outside of a center (freestanding). The magnetic pull of a group of stores usually drives higher customer traffic than a store by itself. The rate of percentage rent to be paid is influenced by the margin of profit of the type of store.

For example, the percentage rents to be paid would be $2,000 if the sales volume of a store reached $490,000 and the breakpoint is $450,000 with a rate of 5 percent of sales ($490,000 − 450,000 =

$40,000 × by 0.05 = $2,000). The natural breakpoint calculation is $22,500 base rent divided by the percentage rent rate of 5 percent = $450,000. The percentage rent rates for various categories of retail can be found in a number of reference books.

Percentage rent may be computed in a number of ways. Some of these are:

1. A cited percentage of gross sales as rent with no guaranteed base rent
2. A cited percentage of gross sales as rent with either a stated guaranteed minimum rent or with a maximum rent (cap)
3. A cited percentage rent rate to be paid (without a limit) over a breakpoint(s) of sales volume.

The variations of these three more common methods could include multiple rates, sales volume ranges, or an application of different rates for various types of sales activity. For example, the tenant shall pay 5 percent of food sales and 8 percent of liquor sales less minimum rent.

The percentage rent clause of a lease is made up of five key components:

1. A percentage rent rate(s)
2. A computation and payment period
3. A definition of gross sales, giving the reportable elements to be included and excluded or deducted from sales
4. A recordkeeping requirement by the tenant
5. A verification process right by the landlord.

Most leases require the tenant to submit a sales report on a monthly, quarterly, or annual basis. These periodic reports are certified by various methods. Some leases might require percentage rent payments at the same time as the sales report is submitted. The annual certified report of sales is required to be certified by either an officer of the tenant or an independent certified public accountant (CPA). Many landlords have developed sample forms for the tenant to use for monthly or annual reports. See Exhibits VII and VIII for sample forms.

The timely submission of sales reports is very critical to a landlord's ability to measure the trends of tenants, categories of tenant, and the center. Reviewing the sales reports of each tenant is very important. Collection of sales reports, including reminder letters, is always helpful in achieving full compliance of timely sales reports. See Exhibit IX for a sample letter.

Sales Analysis Productivity Reports

The accumulation of sales data on each tenant within a center allows management to measure a store's success while better understanding the patterns of the center. There is no better way to gauge the center's current and future needs than the sales performance of its tenants. Management will allocate a sizable amount of human capital to collecting and analyzing sales. As you know now, sales are also important to the center's percentage rent potential revenue. A typical sales analysis report would present current month, this year/last year comparison, percentage changes (both monthly and year-to-date), and percentage (overage) rent projections (monthly and year-to-date). All of this data produces a history of productivity for each store and the overall center, including each category. Planning the leasing and merchandising needs of the center is greatly assisted. Evaluating an individual store while forecasting the five-year plan for the center creates an opportunity for management to maximize the sales of the property. Remember, the higher the sales volumes, the higher the rental income and therefore the value of the center.

Sales and rental data on a square-foot basis are also key. Measuring this can be done on an annual basis or an annualized (rolling twelve-month) basis. Comparative store sales are very helpful to really get a feel of how a store or category is doing. Comp sales would be defined as a store or category that has existed for at least two full years in the same space. Benchmarking these results with the ICSC's Monthly Mall Merchandise Index would provide regional and national trend overlays to your center's/tenant's productivity. See Exhibit X for an example of such a report.

The occupancy cost incurred by a tenant is also a critical component in determining its success or failure. This cost is the total of the base rent, percentage rent, and pass-throughs paid by the tenant. The relationship between these costs and sales, as a percentage, measures the level of financial pressure being experienced by a store. The higher the percentage of occupancy costs to sales, the more likely that a merchant is struggling to achieve profitability. Do not forget that the ability to pay rent and other expenses is directly linked to the volume of sales and the gross profit margin of the store. Certain categories can absorb high percentage of sales relative to occupancy costs. It is suggested that you calculate these percentages for each store, category, section, and level of the center. Some managers have developed a report to look at their stores in this way. The report is known sometimes as the Health Index Report. It may just give you an insight to a potential business failure before one may occur or give you notice that a store's payments are starting to get later and later, which might indicate financial pressures.

While developing the numerous reports to measure and compare the sales, rent, percentage rent, and occupancy costs of the center, remember that these data are only as good as the sources providing it, that is, sales from the tenant and the lease terms. Accuracy and verification of both sources are required to achieve true productivity of a store and value for a center. The verification process of sales reporting will be addressed later in this chapter. Remember, reviewing the lease terms to ensure that they are correctly being invoiced to a tenant is very important to achieve the economic terms agreed to by the parties. This can be done by an internal staff member or by outsourcing the review process. Tenants have continued to examine and verify the pass-through items billed to them by the landlord. The common name for this is a CAM (common-area maintenance) audit or tenant audit.

Ten Other Key Indicators the Tenant Sales Reports Reveal

When stores report sales to the landlord, various insights may be gained. Some of these include:

1. How various retail categories are performing
2. How specific tenants are doing compared to their retail categories
3. Measurement of seasonal performance of tenants versus their retail category norms
4. Sales per square-foot productivity by location within the center
5. Comparable sales versus total sales as the center is continually remerchandised and leased

6. Sales trends on a monthly, annual, and multiyear basis
7. Highlighting of problem tenants
8. Identification of highly productive tenants that should be considered for expansion of space
9. Assistance in forecasting potential percentage (overage) rental income
10. Establishment of guidelines for setting new minimum rents.

Each of the above listed items is a viewpoint to gain knowledge of what is occurring at the center. These sales reports represent a tenant's developed information and are subject to verification by the landlord.

Verification of Tenant Sales Reports

In a shopping center lease in which the tenant is required to pay percentage rent and to report sales, the center management is at risk if it exclusively relies on the reporting of sales by the tenant. The accuracy of reported sales has been shown to be low in comparison to the results of landlords' auditing the sales. The rental payments due by a tenant are directly tied to the reported sales. So the potential is there for the store to understate sales through lease misinterpretation or just miscalculation of the amount due.

The trend that has been observed is that as a company increases its number of stores, it becomes more difficult for it to report sales accurately. Although this may seem counterintuitive, the various gross sales definitions in the numerous leases can be quite different. Standardized methods of reporting do not accurately reflect the actual lease of each store.

What is of real interest is the trend during the 1990s. The frequency of misreporting has increased, as has the error factor (the change in volume) of reported sales compared with final sales after verification by the landlord. This reflects the ongoing pressure that retailers are under as their profit margins shrink and occupancy costs continue to rise. Because rent is a function of sales, the only area of occupancy cost that a retailer can control is the amount of sales being reported, thereby lowering the total rent expense. Lower sales reports mean a decrease in potential percentage rent payments, which affects the net operating income (NOI) of the center. The key to a successful verification program starts with a strong lease clause. See Exhibit XI for some sample language.

The verification process is outlined below:

1. Development of a policy statement
2. Identification of approach—internal, external, or both
3. Establishment of sample size
4. Selection of tenants
5. Notification of tenant's selection
6. Preparation of tenant data package
7. Examination of tenant records
8. Reporting of examination results
9. Follow-up with tenant of the results
10. Maintenance of a record of results.

Tenant selection should be both a qualitative and quantitative process. Risk factors, including sales volumes, breakpoints, rent and occupancy costs, and lease expiration date, are just a few of the telling indicators of stores that qualify as potential audit candidates. A partial listing of the missed opportunities for the sales verification process is included for consideration:

1. Lease renewal or termination
2. Rent-relief request
3. Kick-out performance clause
4. Percent of sales only rental
5. Change of ownership
6. Store closing.

Managing Accounts Receivable and Collection Techniques

The need for accurate billing to tenants is supported by the timely payments of these merchants. A landlord's ability to achieve prompt payments of rents and other amounts reflects its effectiveness in training the tenants to comply with the leases. The functional dimensions of collection include billing or nonbilling by the landlord, tracking of payments received within the accounts receivable system, aging of receivables, and options available to collect past due moneys from the tenant. When a tenant fails to pay an amount due on time, it has violated its lease. You as management should have a written policy on collections so that a consistent approach will be implemented to enforce your leases. Your policy and procedures should reflect the rights and remedies allowed in the leases currently being administered. Be sure you use good legal counsel to establish the methods and techniques to be utilized by your staff. Notices and any other communications need to be handled so that if litigation ultimately takes place, you are on solid ground.

A collection process analysis checklist appears below for review:

1. Does the lease clearly define the amounts to be paid by the tenant?
2. Does the lease contain a timetable for making payments?
3. Does the lease require or allow a penalty or late charge on delinquent payments?
4. Do you use an accounts receivable aging system?
5. What are the delinquent terms used? Current, five days, ten days, twenty days, thirty days, forty-five days, and so on.
6. Are all amounts due the landlord billed to the tenant?
7. Do you have a *written* collection-process policy?
8. Are outstanding accounts' follow-up procedures well defined?

The key to a successful collection program is consistency. Reports that are generated are also important to an effective effort. Toward this end, a typical aging analysis report would include the tenant's name, type of item due, current balance, then several columns citing over thirty days, sixty days, or ninety days. Several Exhibits are shown as examples currently used in the industry.

In summary, the guidelines for collection are as follows:

1. Maintain communication.
2. Achieve promptness.
3. Maintain good records.
4. Develop intelligence.
5. Be consistent.
6. Implement direct action.
7. Establish credibility.
8. Create a surveillance program.

Management's objective is to minimize the bad-debt factor of a center. See Exhibit XIV for some common warning signs.

Benchmarking or Understanding Performance Against Others

Benchmarking is the process of measuring a performance of the business against some standard. The standard can be that of the industry, a competitor, or one within the overall company's performance. By utilizing the standards of other shopping centers in the same trade area or region, management has the opportunity to experience the real objective of the process, which is to learn how to become the best in your field. Ultimately it is a discovery process aimed at exceeding customer expectations. Customers are made up of internal staff and your external customer (the client). Benefits of benchmarking include assisting in identification of topics to benchmark, revealing the strengths and weaknesses of significant processes, improving your understanding of business threats and competitive data, and helping to target current activities that might be reduced or eliminated to improve performance.

Some common standards that might be useful to you include sales productivity, occupancy costs, and average market rents, among others.

One factor to remember is that the type of center you operate and the region of the country you are in will usually result in variations in the data. The closer you are able to match your center to the norms presented, the better the analysis achieved. Do not forget that any larger-size shopping center company will be able to develop its own internal benchmarks to be utilized by staff. As more owners of shopping centers go public and grow as public companies, more information will be available for everyone to use for comparison. The goal is continuous improvement. Benchmarks are also known as models of excellence.

One large company developed a six-step process toward benchmarking:

1. Decide what to benchmark.
2. Plan the benchmarking project.
3. Understand your own performance.
4. Study others.
5. Learn from the data.
6. Use the findings.

Each step requires a team approach, because the educational experience affects the entire organization.

The preparation for a benchmarking study includes a specific process:

1. Obtain management commitment to benchmarking.
2. Identify what should be benchmarked.
3. Create a benchmarking project plan.
4. Identify companies to use as benchmarks.
5. Gather benchmarking information.
6. Know what to do with what you learn.
7. Implement changes that result from benchmarking.

In summary, senior management support is crucial to the success of a benchmarking program. Resources, both financial and human, must be allocated for an effective implementation. The benchmarking study must have clear, accurate objectives based on the customer's requirements. Be ready to address some common problems; for example, people take poor notes, people do not understand the purpose of the study, people are not ready to actually compare variances, and senior management may not actively participate on the teams.

At the end of the process, all members of the organization must begin or continue to think in terms of systems, not just a specific task. Benchmarking enables you to improve internally by learning from external resources. Everyone should strive to do his or her best and help the company become the next model of excellence. The ultimate goal of exceeding customer expectations will occur as a result of learning the organization goal of improving every day.

The financial implications of decision making today directly affect the value of the shopping center. You have now reviewed a broad range of concepts regarding a shopping center. Utilization of these tools should assist you for a long time to come.

Kenneth S. Lamy is President of The Lamy Group, Ltd., New Orleans, Louisiana.

EXHIBIT I
Lease Summary Report
As of January, 1997

Tenant Name Suite/Tenant Type Sq Ft/Alt Sq Ft Floor	LS Begin LS End Term	TOTAL BASE RENT Date Changes	Amount	Amt/SF	CPI % % Applied % Cap	FREE RENT Begins	Months	RECOVERIES Name(s) Total Stop/SF	TENANT IMPROVEMENTS Amount Amt/SF	LEASING COMM Amount Amt/SF	PERCENT RENT Breakpoint Begin Sales Pct/Cap	RENEWAL ASSUMPTION Option/Renewal/Spec Spec Profits Spec Renewal Prob
101/Exet Off 50,000 SF/0 ASF 1st Floor	Jan. 1990 Dec. 1993 5 yr 0 mo Base	Jan. 1993	$750,000 $900,000	$15.00 $18.00	None	Jan. 1990	6 mo Upfront	Fixed and Variable $5.49	$1,150,000 $23.00	$477,461 $9.55	None	Option
1.05/Exet Off 50,000 SF/0 ASF 1st Floor	May 1989 Dec. 1995 5 yr 0 mo Base	May 1989	$850,000	$17.00	CPI Growth Rate 50% 4.0%	May 1989	6 mo Upfront	Fixed and Variable None	None	$40,000 $.80	None	Speculative Office Tenant Prof 75%
1.10/Exet Off 5.000 SF/0 ASF 1st Floor	Jan. 1990 Dec. 1995 6 yr 0 mo Option	Jan. 1990 Jul. 1991 Jan. 1993 Jul. 1994	$75,000 $77,500 $80,500 $81,750	$15.00 $15.50 $16.10 $16.25	None	Jan. 1990 Jul. 1990 Jan. 1991	1 mo 1 mo 5 mo	None	$75,000 $15.00	None	Natural $900,000 7.00%/Unlimited	None
120/Spec Off 15,000 SF/0 ASF 1st Floor	May 1991 Apr. 1995 4 yr 0 mo Base	May 1991	$262,650	$17.51	CPI Growth Rate 100% None	May 1991	3 mo Upfront	Fixed and Variable $5.64	$231,750 $15.45	$59,096 $3.94	None	Speculative Office Tenant Prof 75%
5 Spec Office Tenant #2 120/Spec Off 15,000 SF/0 ASF 1st Floor	Oct. 1991 Sep. 1996 5 yr 0 mo Base	Oct. 1991	$262,650	$17.51	CPI Growth Rate 100% None	Oct. 1991	3 mo Upfront	Fixed and Variable $5.86	$231,750 $15.45	$74,855 $4.99	None	Speculative Office Tenant Prof 75%
6 Spec Office Tenant #3 140/Spec Off 15,000 SF/0 ASF 1st Floor	Mar. 1992 Feb. 1997 5 yr 0 mo Base	Mar. 1992	$270,529	$18.04	CPI Growth Rate 100% None	Mar. 1992	3 mo Upfront	Fixed and Variable $5.97	$238,702 $15.91	$77,101 $5.14	None	Speculative Office Tenant Prof 75%
Total Square Feet Total Alt Square Feet	150,000 0											

EXHIBIT II
Lease Summary Report

Name:				Lease Number:		
Start Date:	5/1/1997			LSF:	5000	
End Date:	4/30/2002			RSF:	5200	
Floor:	1			Space Type:	Signed	
Space:	1			Lease Type:	Signed	

Base Rent:

Method	Amount	Rate Item	Tax Rate	Abatements: Date	Months	Free Days
Input—$ Amount	180,000.00	180	0.00	5/1/1997	0.00	180.00

Recovery Data:

Recovery Type	Recov Method	Expense Item	Starting Amt	Free Days	Basis	Prp Shr/Factor	Base Date	Base Amount	Cap Method	Cap Amount
Expense	Net	Operating	0.00	180.00	GLA	2.00		0.00		0.00
Expense	Net	Real Estate Tax	0.00	180.00	GLA	2.10		0.00		0.00

Percent Rent

Sales Item	Method	Free Days	Breakpoints Amt/SF	Percentage		Overage Caps Sales/SF	Recov. Item	Method	Pct
Food Sales	Pct Rent-Exc Rnt	180.00	100.00	8.00		0.00	Operating	Cap	0.00
			115.00	6.00					

Tenant Improvements Method	Amount	Rate Item	Month	Pct	Commissions Method	Amount	Rate Item	Month	Pct
	50.00		0.00	60.00		25.00		0.00	33.33
			6.00	20.00				12.00	66.67
			12.00	20.00					

Renewals

Method	Vac Item	Repeat		Renewal Lse	Vac Days
No Renewal		No			

EXHIBIT III

The Mall

Current Rent Roll As Of 12/01/97

| Tenant | Space | Area | Terms | RENT | | | | PERCENTAGE RENT | | RECOVERIES | | OPTIONS CLAUSES | | | |
				From	To	Annual Rent	PSF	%	Breakpoint	CAM	TAX	Effective	From	To	Rate
	A2–13	1,135	03/01/91– 02/28/01	03/01/91	02/28/94	54,000.00	47.58	6.00	900,000	PR	PR				
				03/01/94	02/28/98	60,000.00	52.86	6.00	1,000,000						
				03/01/98	02/28/01	66,000.00	58.15	6.00	1,100,000						
	B1–01	1,612	03/01/95– 02/28/05	03/01/95	02/28/98	88,659.96	55.00	6.00	1,477,666	PR	PR				
				03/01/98	02/28/02	96,720.00	60.00	6.00	1,612,000						
				03/01/02	02/28/05	104,780.04	65.00	6.00	1,746,334						
	B1–03	1,065	04/15/90– 04/30/98	04/15/90	02/28/91	42,600.00	40.00	8.00	532,500	PR	PR				
				03/01/91	08/31/91	0.00	0.00	8.00							
				09/01/91	04/14/92	42,600.00	40.00	8.00	532,500						
				04/15/92	04/30/96	47,925.00	45.00	8.00	599,063						
				05/01/96	04/30/98	53,250.00	50.00	8.00	665,625						
	B1–05	2,289	11/10/88– 01/31/99	11/10/88	01/31/99	51,503.04	22.50	5.00	1,030,061	PR	PR				
	B1–07	3,424	04/14/92– 05/31/02	04/14/92	04/14/95	82,176.00	24.00	4.00	2,054,400	PR	PR				
				04/15/95	04/14/99	89,024.04	26.00	4.00	2,225,598						
				04/15/99	05/31/02	95,871.96	28.00	4.00	2,396,799						
	B1–11	7,599	09/15/94– 01/31/05	09/15/94	09/14/96	0.00	0.00	5.00	3,039,600	PR	PR				
				09/15/96	01/31/05	151,980.00	20.00	5.00	3,039,600						
	B1–15	4,408	03/01/95– 02/28/05	03/01/95	02/28/05	88,159.92	20.00	5.00	1,763,198	PR/C	PR				

Total Building

	Area	%	# Of Units
Occupied Sq ft:	1,134,170	100.0%	156
Vacant Sq ft:	0	0.0%	0
Total:	1,134,170	100.0%	156

776,737.35 — Current Monthly Rent
9,320,848.20 — Annualized Current Monthly Rent
9,114,510.89 — Actual Rent Charges For The Next 12 Months

*indicates that the space has been vacated early by the tenant (not included in the Occupied Sq ft) but is still being billed

ESCALATION/RECOVERY CODES
PR   Tenant pays a full pro rata share of expenses (tenant reimburses landlord for all expenses)
PR/C   Tenant pays a capped pro rata share of expenses
BY##   Tenant pays its pro rata share of expenses over a base (where ## represents the last two digits of the base year)
BY##/C   Tenant pays a capped pro rata share of the expenses over a base (where ## represents the last two digits of the base year)
NNN   Triple net (all expenses paid directly to vendors by tenant)
MODN   Modified net (tenant pays only utilities and janitorial directly, all others are paid as a full pro rata share)

EXHIBIT IV
Leasing Status

	12/31/96		12/31/97		09/30/98	
	Area (Sq. Ft.)	Percent of Total	Area (Sq. Ft.)	Percent of Total	Area (Sq. Ft.)	Percent of Total
Center						
Leased						
Available						
Total						
Outparcels						
Leased						
Available		%		%		%
Total						
Total						

EXHIBIT V
Rental Trends

	1996	1997	1998 Actual (through 9/30/98)	Forecast (Annual)
Leased (%, End of Period)*				
Area Leased (Sq. Ft.)				
Effective Rent (Per Sq. Ft.)				
Tenant Work (Per Sq. Ft.)				

Note: The effective rent and tenant work figures are weighted averages for leased executed during the period.

EXHIBIT VI
Lease Expiration Summary

Year	No. of Tenants	AREA		TOTAL RENT	
		Sq. Ft.	Cumulative % of Property	Rent	Cumulative % of Property
Vacant	13	15,733	3.78%	0	0.00%
12/31/95	3	4,384	4.84%	117,091	1.41%
12/31/96	7	13,418	8.06%	342,881	5.56%
12/31/97	49	114,430	35.58%	2,135,927	31.36%
12/31/98	12	22,273	40.94%	575,640	38.32%
12/31/99	6	20,476	45.86%	401,228	43.16%
12/31/00	8	8,502	47.90%	344,387	47.32%
12/31/01	4	3,876	48.84%	113,937	48.70%
12/31/02	10	21,691	54.05%	707,094	57.24%
12/31/03	8	27,094	60.57%	538,649	63.75%
12/31/04	7	18,241	64.95%	452,386	69.22%
12/31/05	9	28,482	71.80%	710,400	77.80%
12/31/06	12	69,956	88.62%	1,187,584	92.15%
12/31/08	2	47,306	100.00%	649,987	100.00%
TOTAL	150	415,862	100.00%	8,277,192	100.00%

Anchor/Outparcel Expiration

Anchor	Area Sq. Ft.	Lease Expiration	Operating Covenant Expiration*
Outparcel			n/a
			n/a
			n/a

*In general, the Reciprocal Operating Agreement (REA) requires each anchor to operate for fifteen years under its existing trade name and then for five more years as a retail department store.

EXHIBIT VII
Shopping Center
Gross Sales Reporting Form

Tenant Name: _________________________________ Month/Year: _____________

Tenant address: ____

____

Gross sales for the period $_____________________

   Less: Authorized deductions   ($____________________)

Gross sales
   Subject to percentage rent $_____________________

Percentage rent rate   _____________________%

Percentage rent for the period $_____________________

   Less: Minimum base rent   ($____________________)

Percentage rent payable $_____________________
   (enclosed check when applicable)

Please submit this report to: ____

I hereby certify that the above is a true and complete statement of the gross sales made form the premises at the above location for the month stated and that the calculations are made in accordance with the methods provided in the lease for the premises indicated.

_______________________________   _______________________________

Authorized signature   Date

____

Title

EXHIBIT VIII
Annual Certified Sales Statement

Date ________________

To: ____

    RE: Store- ________________________________

This is to certify that gross sales for the period of ____________________, 19______ through

____________________, 19______ are as follows:

JANUARY	$________________
FEBRUARY	$________________
MARCH	$________________
APRIL	$________________
MAY	$________________
JUNE	$________________
JULY	$________________
AUGUST	$________________
SEPTEMBER	$________________
OCTOBER	$________________
NOVEMBER	$________________
DECEMBER	$________________
GROSS SALES	$________________

I hereby certify that the above-stated gross sales are accurate and correct to the best of my knowledge.

____
Authorized signature

____
Title

NOTE: This statement may be utilized if store does not generate its own company statement.

EXHIBIT IX

April 8, 1999

Mr. Joe Smith
Store Manager
Universal Mall
1234 Any Street
Any Town, USA 10001

Dear Tenant;

To date, we have not received your written sales report for the period ending __________.

In accordance with Section 4.3 C of your Lease, the Tenant shall furnish to the Landlord the above-mentioned statement signed and verified by the Tenant within 15 days after the end of each calendar month.

In the event this report is not received within the specified period, it will be necessary to audit your books and records in order to determine such figures. The cost of this audit will be borne by the Tenant under the General Default provisions of the Lease.

Your prompt cooperation and attention in this matter is appreciated.

Very truly yours,

Jane Smith
Mall Manager

EXHIBIT X

Gross Sales Report: Arranged in Property, Retail Category Sequence for ______________________
(Shopping Center)

Category/ Tenant Name	Sq. Ft.	1st Level Percentage	Annual Breakpoints	Reports	(Month) (Year) Current	Sq. Ft.	(Month) (Year) Last Year	Sq. Ft.	% Change	YTD Current Year Sales	YTD Last Year Sales	% Change	Sales/ Sq. Ft. TRLG Ave.
Category Totals													
Category Totals													
Category Totals													
Category Totals													
Category Totals													

EXHIBIT XI
Sample Language
Right to Audit Tenant's Records

Tenant shall utilize, and cause to be utilized by sub-tenants, concessionaires, and licensees, cash registers equipped with sealed continuous totals to record all sales in the presence of the customer at time of sale, and Tenant shall keep on the Leased Premises or its main offices for at least thirty-six (36) months after expiration of each Lease Year or Partial Lease Year records conforming to sound accounting practices showing all of the Gross Sales made by Tenant or others at, in, from, and upon the Leased Premises for such Lease Year or Partial Lease Year, including but not limited to all federal, state, and local tax returns relating to Gross Sales, daily cash register, and Point-of-Sale tapes, retained detail continuous tapes, sales slips, daily sales reports, cash receipts, the original records of all orders accepted by means of electronic, telephonic, video, computer, or other technology-based system, and sales journals, disbursement journals, general ledgers, chart of accounts, back statements including deposit slips, financial statements, and other support documents related to Gross Sales.

Landlord shall have the right from time to time by its accountants or representatives to audit all statements of Gross Sales and in connection with such audits to examine all records (including all supporting data and all tax records) of Gross Sales, and Tenant shall provide, make, or cause each sub-tenant, concessionaire, and licensee to provide all such records readily available for such examination. Landlord or its representatives shall have the right to copy any and all records of Tenant, sub-Tenant, concessionaire, and licensee supporting their examination of Gross Sales. If Landlord's accountant or representative determines that sufficient documentation is not maintained, retained, recorded, or available to verify Tenant's actual Gross Sales as hereinafter defined, Tenant shall pay for the cost of such examination and, in addition, should Landlord deem it necessary, Tenant shall pay any such other additional fees for a reconstruction of records for the determination of Gross Sales of Tenant for any period being audited. If any such audit discloses that the actual Gross Sales differ from those reported, Tenant shall forthwith pay the cost of such audit, percentage rents due, if any, along with interest charges at eighteen percent (18%) per annum or the maximum rate allowed. If such audit discloses that said Gross Sales exceeded those reported by more than three percent (3%), Landlord shall, in addition to the foregoing rights, have the right to terminate this Lease. In the event Tenant overreports its Gross Sales and is due a refund, Tenant will be granted a credit toward future rents after first deducting the cost of the examination. If such Audit shall disclose that Tenant's records, in landlord's determination, are inadequate to disclose such Gross Sales, then in addition to any and all other remedies available to it herein, Landlord shall be entitled to collect as Additional Rent an amount equal to fifty percent (50%) of the Annual Minimum Rent payable by Tenant during the period in question.

If Tenant fails to attain Gross Sales sufficient to incur Percentage Rent in any Lease Year following the second full Lease Year during the primary term, then Landlord may terminate this Lease by notice to Tenant given within six (6) months after the end of such Lease Year and this Lease shall terminate ninety (90) days thereafter.

EXHIBIT XII
Model Letter

Insist on Prompt Rent Payments

If you have a tenant who has been paying rent late, reestablish your right to on-time rent payments by sending a letter telling the tenant to pay promptly in the future. This Model Letter is based on one used by Toronto attorney Stephen J. Messinger. The letter assumes that you have a provision in your lease requiring prompt payment of rent. Talk to your attorney about adapting this letter to fit your circumstances.

Nov. 1, 1996

John Tenant
ABC Store, XYZ Mall
Anytown, USA 00000

Dear Mr. Tenant,

Section 4 of your lease requires you to pay your rent in full by the first of the month. You have been consistently late in paying rent for the past few months. We have accepted late rent payments as a courtesy to you, not as a modification of your lease.

This letter will serve notice to you that as of Dec. 1, 1996, you must follow the terms of your lease requiring monthly rent payments to be made by the first of the month.

Any payment made after the due date will be considered late and a breach of the lease. If a rent payment is made late, we reserve the right to take all proper legal action against you pursuant to the lease and the laws of this state.

If you have any questions, do not hesitate to call us. We look forward to your cooperation.

Yours truly,
Jane Manager

EXHIBIT XIII
Accounts Receivable Aging Report

Tenant	Total	Current	30–60 Days	61–90 Days	91+ Days	Comments
Total						

EXHIBIT XIV
Bad-Debt Warning Signals

Effective management of receivables is essential for healthy cash flow. You can make your job easier if you are aware of some of the warning signals that indicate your customers may be having trouble meeting their obligations.

1. **Watch for erratic payment trends.** For example, irregular lump-sum payments on accounts rather than payment of the invoice amount may indicate that the merchant is in financial difficulty and paying "as much as possible when I've got it." Preventive measures might include lowering the credit line, making future sales COD, or holding future shipments until the outstanding balance is paid in full.

2. **Be alert to "red flags" such as postdated checks and unsigned checks.** While the latter may appear inadvertent, they may really be a delaying tactic.

3. **Beware of established companies that have never done business with you in the past switching to your firm without a good reason.** They may be switching to you because they have credit problems elsewhere. Check their references carefully.

4. **Watch for industry trends, such as an increase in the number of bankruptcies.** If bankruptcies are increasing in your industry or in related fields, you should watch your own receivables with extra care.

5. **Be alert for news of litigation involving your retailers.** Some metropolitan newspapers report bankruptcy filings, and *The Dun's Bulletin* will make you aware of some other cases.

Glossary

accounting period   The amount of time covered by an operating statement; generally, a month, a quarter, or a year (which is called a fiscal year or, if it ends on December 31, a calendar year).

accounts   The detailed description of a company's assets, liabilities, equity, revenues, and expenses.

accounts payable   Cash amounts owed on open accounts, whereby the buyer pays cash sometime after the date of sale.

accounts receivable   Cash amounts billed to customers and still owed by them.

accrual   The entry made to record a bill not yet received or an income item not yet collected.

accrual basis method of accounting   An accounting method that, unlike the cash basis method, recognizes the impact of transactions on financial statements in the time periods when revenues (earnings) and expenses (costs) are incurred instead of when they are actually received or paid.

accrued liabilities   Amounts recognized for wages, salaries, interest, and similar items not yet payable.

accumulated depreciation   The portion of the original cost of fixed assets that has already been charged to operations as an expense.

administration fee   The cost of actually administering the common area of a shopping center; a standard addition to the overall cost of common-area maintenance (CAM), typically set at 15 percent but often heavily negotiated.

amortization   The repayment of a portion of the principal before the end of the term of the loan; the opposite of an interest-only loan; such expenses, related to intangible assets, are recorded on an operating statement after net operating income (NOI), or "below the (bottom) line."

appraisal   The way in which the value of a property is determined.

appraisal rent   An amount based on sales potential as affected by the appraisal of a property at a given point in time; sometimes used interchangeably with *market rent*.

assets   Economic resources expected to benefit a business's future activities; the things that a business owns and uses for its operations, with a useful life greater than a year.

asset turnover   A ratio determined by dividing net sales by average total assets.

audit trail   An explicit set of documentation by accountants illustrating how each entry made its way into the books.

balance sheet   The portion of a financial statement showing a company's financial position—its assets, liabilities, and equity—at a particular point in time, analogous to a scorecard. On a balance sheet, assets equal liabilities plus equity; equity equals assets minus liabilities.

base rent   *see* **minimum rent**

benchmarking   The process of measuring a business's performance in a particular area against some standard, which can be that of the industry as a whole, that of a competitor, or one related to the same business's overall performance.

bottom line   A measurement of profit (or loss) in a budget, expressed as net operating income (NOI), as earnings before interest, taxes, depreciation, and amortization (EBITDA), or as funds from operations (FFO).

breakpoint   Theoretically, the point at which a tenant breaks even on expenses and sales, and thereafter begins to make a profit (a percentage of which is sometimes required to be paid to the landlord); also called a *sales breakpoint* or *natural breakpoint.*

budgeted rent   An amount based on sales potential, and representing the target approved by ownership for its annual plan; sometimes used interchangeably with *market rent.*

business plan   A detailed, carefully prepared road map for the operation of a business for the coming year or years; it sets a direction and destination (strategy) for the business and plots the course (tactics) to get there.

CAM   *see* **common-area maintenance**

cap   A maximum amount that a tenant must pay for certain expenses, no matter how much they actually increase; usually a set amount or a percentage of increase.

cap (capitalization) rate   The ratio of income to price, determined by such factors as the market and the quality of a property, and used along with net operating income (NOI) to determine value; the cap rate equals net operating income (NOI) divided by value.

capital expenditures   Payments for something expected to last for at least a year, and recorded on a balance sheet as assets; for a shopping center, these include tenant allowances, work by the landlord to improve a space, and commissions paid to the broker or management company.

cash basis method of accounting   An accounting method that, unlike the accrual basis method, recognizes revenues and expenses as they are actually received or paid, not as they are earned or owed.

cash flow   The amount of spendable income available after all payments have been made for operating expenses and mortgage principal and interest; it is a way of recognizing the timing of receipts and payments.

chart of accounts   An organized list of a company's financial activity codes, the "financial DNA."

closing entries   Special entries in a journal, made to reverse all account balances in preparation for the next accounting period.

collateral   Generally, the guaranteed backup source of a loan repayment if the investor does not repay the loan as specified in the loan documents; this security ranges from property to a personal guarantee.

common-area maintenance (CAM)   The charge to a tenant for a share of the costs of maintaining a common area in a shopping center, including cleaning, security, and utilities.

comparative lease analysis   A method of quantifying the economic differences between a proposed lease and a baseline, such as the development pro forma, for the same space.

Consumer Price Index (CPI)   A U.S. government indicator of rising prices, used to measure the impact of inflation on consumers; this information, based on a broad survey of a large and widely varied number of items, is updated and published by the U.S. Bureau of Labor Statistics at the end of every month.

contra-asset account   An account on a balance sheet that complements an asset account; additions to this type of account are recorded as credits, in the right-hand column.

cost of capital   Generally expressed as the interest rate one must pay to borrow the necessary capital to make an investment. If the capital is already available, the cost of the capital is the opportunity cost in terms of not being able to use that amount for alternative investments.

CPI   *see* **Consumer Price Index**

credit loss   The expected percentage of revenue that will be lost from one or more tenants due to nonpayment, or noncollection, of rent.

credits   Entered in the right-hand column of each account, these are additions to a liability account, an equity account, or a revenue account, or reductions in an asset account or an expense account.

credit tenants   Generally, national chains with strong financial statements, to which an appraiser might apply a different rate, based on lower risk, than to smaller, local operators.

cross-collateralization   The concept that each of the partners in a property with more than one owner is personally responsible for full repayment of a loan, even though each partner may own only a small percentage of the property. It also applies to a group of properties covered by multiple loans, in which case the income from—or even the sale of—other properties in the group may be required to comply with the loan terms of any one of those properties.

current asset   Cash and other assets that are reasonably expected to be converted to cash or sold or consumed within one year.

current liabilities   Usually debts that fall due within the coming year or within the normal operating cycle if longer than a year; also referred to as *short-term debt.*

current ratio   The ratio of current assets to current liabilities; a current ratio of 2:1 (meaning two dollars of current assets for every dollar of current liabilities) is generally considered adequate.

debentures   Debts, such as bonds, notes, and loans, that are formal certificates of indebtedness indicating a company's promise to pay interest at a specified annual rate.

debits   Entered in the left-hand column of each account, these are additions to an asset account or an expense account, or reductions in a liability account.

debt coverage ratio   The relationship between projected net operating income and expected debt service, expressed as NOI divided by debt service. A ratio of 1.0 (NOI equals debt service) means there is no margin of error, because any drop in NOI will leave insufficient cash to pay the debt service. The higher the ratio, the higher the margin of error, and the greater the chance that the loan will be repaid.

debt-to-equity ratio   An indicator of whether a company is using debt excessively, this is calculated by dividing total liabilities by total equity.

depreciation   Expenses, or lost value over time, related to tangible assets; this is recorded on an operating statement after net operating income (NOI), or "below the (bottom) line."

discounted cash flow   The principle that a dollar in the hand today is worth more than the same amount received in the future.

discount rate   The rate that measures return on investment compared with a risk-free rate of return such as that of U.S. Treasury notes; crucial in determining lease value.

double-entry bookkeeping The foundation of bookkeeping, this refers to the fact that for every addition, there must be a subtraction, so that the totals remained balanced; credits and debits are listed in columns under the name of each account.

EBITDA An acronym for *e*arnings *b*efore *i*nterest, *t*axes, *d*epreciation, and *a*mortization, this approximates the total cash from operations; used in the supplemental disclosures accompanying a financial statement, it is an attempt by analysts to measure a company's operations by eliminating certain charges (such as depreciation) and focusing on the results from operations without either interest revenue or expense.

equities Claims against, or interest in, an entity's assets.

equity The owner's interest in a company after all obligations are met; analogous to the difference between the value of your home and the balance of your mortgage.

expenses What a company pays out to make a product or deliver a service; for example, the cost of utilities in a shopping center.

FFO *see* **funds from operations**

FIFO *see* **first in, first out**

financial statement A summarized report of accounting transactions, composed of the balance sheet, the operating (or income) statement, and the statement of cash flows.

first in, first out (FIFO) An accounting method that assumes inventory acquired earliest is sold or used up first. Thus, the "Monday" inventory item is deemed to have been sold before the "Tuesday" item, regardless of which actual item is delivered to the customer. In times of rising prices, use of this method usually results in the largest gross profits.

fiscal year Any twelve-month period for a lease (or any other financial purpose), such as July to June; if it is from January 1 to December 31, it is called a *calendar year.*

fixed assets *see* **tangible assets**

fixed rate An interest rate set at the time of a loan and unchanging over the life of the loan.

floating rate   An interest rate that fluctuates over the life of a loan, based on some relationship to a benchmark such as a bank's prime lending rate.

funds from operations (FFO)   A measurement favored by real estate investment trusts (REITs) that approximates the cash-generating power of a company; analogous to net operating income (NOI), it consists of net income, excluding gains (or losses) from debt restructuring and sales of property, plus depreciation and amortization after adjustments for unconsolidated partnerships and joint ventures.

future value (FV)   A way of determining the eventual value of an investment, based on the amount of the initial investment, the reinvestment rate, and the number of years under consideration; analogous to figuring out how much a bank account paying a particular interest rate will be worth after a set number of years.

FV   *see* **future value**

GAAP   An acronym for *g*enerally *a*ccepted *a*ccounting *p*rinciples; an authoritative set of rules, adopted by the accounting profession, that dictates the way a business reports its financial condition and performance.

GAFO   An acronym referring to sales of *g*eneral merchandise, *a*pparel, *f*urniture and home furnishings, and *o*ther shopper goods.

general ledger   The place—in a book or, today, in a computer—where an accountant or bookkeeper records, collects, and stores all accounts; also called a *ledger*.

generally accepted accounting principles   *see* **GAAP**

GLA   *see* **gross leasable area**

goodwill   The excess of the cost of an acquired company over the sum of the fair-market values of its identifiable assets less its liabilities.

gross income   Revenues before any expenses are deducted.

gross leasable area (GLA)   The total area in a shopping center on which tenants pay rent, including storage and miscellaneous space as well as selling space; the total area in a center that produces income.

gross lease A lease in which the tenant pays one flat amount and the landlord pays all other expenses of the shopping center, such as taxes, insurance, and property repairs and maintenance.

gross margin A ratio measuring the difference between sales and total cost of goods sold.

gross potential revenue A figure used by appraisers to determine potential revenue, based on 100 percent occupancy.

hard costs The brick-and-mortar elements of a redevelopment project, such as the land, the building, and building improvements.

hurdle rate An investor's minimum acceptable rate of return.

HVAC An acronym for *h*eating, *v*entilation, and *a*ir-conditioning needs, taken care of in a shopping center by large, powerful machines.

income statement *see* **operating statement.**

intangible assets A class of long-lived assets that are not physical in nature; they are the rights to expected future benefits deriving from their acquisition and continued possession. Examples include tenant allowances, goodwill, franchises, patents, trademarks, and copyrights.

interest-only loan A type of loan, preferred by borrowers, in which there is no amortization—no principal is paid back prior to the maturity of the loan.

interest rate The additional return required by the lender to make a given loan, paid on a regular basis.

internal controls The safeguards a company puts in place to help detect accounting errors and prevent employee dishonesty on financial statements.

internal rate of return (IRR) A discount rate at which the present value (PV) of projected cash flow exactly equals the initial investment.

inventory turnover A ratio measuring the adequacy and efficiency of the inventory balance, calculated by dividing the cost of goods sold by the amount of the average inventory.

IRR *see* **internal rate of return**

jointly and severally   *see* **cross-collateralization**

journal entry   A process of recording detailed information about accounts in a journal.

journals   Books used to record the original entries and details of various accounts; totals are then transferred to the general ledger.

last in, first out (LIFO)   An accounting method that assumes inventory acquired most recently is sold or used up first. This treats the most recent costs as the costs of goods sold, unlike FIFO, which associates the most recent costs with inventories. Many accountants believe that LIFO provides a more realistic income picture, because net income measured using LIFO combines current sales prices and current acquisition costs.

lease   The document that establishes all of the ground rules, both financial and nonfinancial, between landlord and tenant; specifically, a signed agreement that transfers the right to the possession and use of a property to a tenant for a definite period of time, establishes the responsibilities of the landlord and the tenant, sets standards, and states what is recoverable from the tenant for the maintenance process.

lease abstract   A short version of a lease, containing the most important facts about it in order to facilitate later reviews (for example, by new employees).

ledger   *see* **general ledger**

liabilities   A business's economic obligations to nonowners; what a company owes.

LIFO   *see* **last in, first out**

liquidity   The ease with which an investment of any kind can be converted to cash. A simple bank account, for example, is more liquid than real estate.

long-term liabilities   *see* **noncurrent liabilities**

marginal cost of capital   *see* **risk premium**

market rent   Properly, an amount based on sales potential rather than what is necessary to produce a desired return on investment or to cover development costs; the rate at which space would be leased if offered in a current competitive market; sometimes used interchangeably with *budgeted rent* or *appraisal rent.*

minimum rent   The basic rent that a tenant will pay the landlord each year, in twelve equal, consecutive installments, computed based on an amount of rent per square foot; also called *base rent.*

natural breakpoint   *see* **breakpoint**

negotiated inducements   Any incentives offered by a landlord to persuade a tenant to commit to a lease. As known factors that will definitely occur, such as tenant construction allowances or free rent periods, these are quantifiable in terms of amount and timing.

net income   The difference between total income and total expenses.

net lease   A lease in which the tenant agrees to pay not only rent but also a share of other expenses, such as taxes, insurance, and property repairs and maintenance.

net operating income (NOI)   The difference between a business's revenues (or gross income) and its operating expenses (such as property taxes, insurance, utilities, management fees, heating and cooling expenses, repairs, and maintenance fees), and used in determining a company's value (which equals NOI divided by the company's cap rate); more likely to be listed as a line item in a company's internal operating statements than as an entry in the operating statement that is part of a 10K or an audited financial statement.

net present value (NPV)   A method of calculating present value for multiple payments made in different future years and bringing together all of these amounts into today's dollars. A higher discount rate means a smaller NPV.

NOI   *see* **net operating income**

noncash charges   Depreciation and amortization; the amounts recorded in these accounts represent economic value received in the current year from an asset, not expenditures in the current accounting period.

noncurrent liabilities   Debts that fall due beyond one year; also called *long-term liabilities.*

nonrecourse loans   A type of loan, preferred by borrowers, in which the lender can look only to the sale of a property as the source of repayment of a loan, not to the borrower's other assets, if the loan is not repaid.

NPV   *see* **net present value**

occupancy cost ratio   A comparison of a retailer's annual sales volume to its annual occupancy costs (including base rent, real estate taxes, common-area maintenance, or CAM, building insurance, marketing/promotion funds, and percentage rent), expressed as a percentage.

operating budget   The portion of a business plan that generally deals with the upcoming year, as opposed to the longer-term strategic plan; sometimes simply called a *budget.*

operating cost ratio   The complement of the operating margin, frequently used by analysts; the two add up to 100 percent.

operating expenses   All expenses, occurring periodically, used to produce the sales or revenue of a company, except for depreciation.

operating margin   A ratio measuring the operational efficiency of a company, this is calculated by dividing operating income by net sales; the result describes what percentage of every dollar of sales was retained as profit from operations.

operating statement   The portion of a financial statement showing, by specific categories, the revenues earned by a business, the expenses incurred in earning the revenues, and the resulting net income or loss (revenue minus expense) for the current accounting period; also called an *income statement* or a *profit-and-loss statement (P&L),* and generally produced on a monthly, quarterly, or annual basis.

overage rent   Percentage rent paid on gross sales in excess of a stated breakpoint for that tenant.

percentage rent   An amount of rent paid annually, in addition to the tenant's minimum base rent, based on a percentage of gross sales; the rate is defined in the lease.

personal guarantee   *see* **recourse basis**

posting   The process of transferring information from a journal to a general ledger; when posting to the general ledger, there must be a credit for every debit and vice versa.

prepaid expenses   Advance payments to suppliers. Examples include prepaid rent and insurance. They belong in current assets, because if they were not present, more cash would be needed to conduct current operations.

present value (PV)   Unlike future value (FV), this is a calculation that relies on the discount rate to determine what the present value of a known future amount of money should be.

probability distribution   A compilation of all potential outcomes of a transaction, along with the probability, or degree of certainty, that each will occur—ranging from zero, or no possibility, to one, or complete certainty. The sum of all values in such a distribution must equal one.

profit-and-loss statement (P&L)   *see* **operating statement**

pro forma   A developer's estimates of all costs of planning, developing, building, and operating a shopping center, an expansion, or a redevelopment. Based on estimates of revenue and expense, the developer is able to compute anticipated net income and projected value.

property, plant, and equipment   *see* **tangible assets**

pro rata   In proportion, according to some exactly calculable factor.

PV   *see* **present value**

quick assets   What is available to cover a sudden emergency—in other words, readily available cash; determined by taking current assets and deducting inventories, prepaid expenses, and any other illiquid current assets (ones that cannot be readily converted to cash).

quick ratio   A ratio determined by dividing quick assets by current liabilities; the result measures the adequacy of available working capital.

quote rates   The rates calculated for common-area maintenance (CAM), real estate taxes, and other charges based on budgeted expense and budgeted occupancy.

rate of retention   The rate at which existing tenants renew their leases in their existing spaces.

rates The tenant's share of add-on charges, stated on a per-square-foot basis.

receivable collection A ratio determined by dividing average accounts receivable by net sales over 365 days.

recourse basis A type of loan, preferred by lenders, that obliges the borrower to use personal assets as a secondary means to repay a loan, if the proceeds from a sale of the property are not sufficient to cover the amount owed on the loan; often referred to as a *personal guarantee.*

recovery ratio The relationship between related revenue and expense.

reinvestment rate The rate at which an investment will grow each year, analogous to the interest rate on a bank account; used to determine future value (FV).

REIT An acronym for a *real estate investment trust,* a relatively recent means of ownership of shopping centers and other properties.

rent leveling A purely accounting process by which average rent is deemed income in each year throughout a lease, regardless of the actual schedule of payments.

rent roll A summary schedule listing of all spaces in a shopping center, vacant as well as occupied, for quick reference and full disclosure. Information listed here includes tenant names, retail category, size of each store, fixed minimum annual rent, the term of each lease (including commencement and expiration dates), the annual breakpoint for each tenant, and the percentage rent rate(s), as well as other information.

rent steps The scheduled increases in rent that are specified in a tenant's lease, and budgeted in the appropriate month.

retained earnings This represents the profit or loss held in a company, based on accumulated income minus whatever is distributed to stockholders or transferred to capital accounts; also referred to as *retained income.*

retained income *see* **retained earnings**

return on assets A ratio calculated by dividing net income by average total assets.

return-on-equity (ROE) ratio   A measurement of profitability, often used as return on investment (ROI), and calculated by dividing net income by the average equity over a two-year period; this ratio helps an investor determine if a business would make an attractive investment.

return on investment (ROI)   The amount that goes to the owner beyond the return of the investment's capital.

return on sales   A ratio determined by dividing net income by net sales.

revenue growth   A ratio determined by dividing the difference between this year's net sales and last year's net sales by the amount of last year's net sales.

revenues   What a company receives for its products or services; for a shopping center, its rents and other charges paid by tenants.

risk premium   The difference between a discount rate and a risk-free, or safe, rate of return such as that of a U.S. Treasury note; this factor, often referred to as the *marginal cost of capital,* compensates the investor for inherent market risks, business risks, portfolio management, and loss of liquidity.

ROE   *see* **return-on-equity ratio**

ROI   *see* **return on investment**

sales breakpoint   *see* **breakpoint**

short-term debt   *see* **current liabilities**

soft costs   Architectural fees, interest on loans, payroll, and indirect expenses in a redevelopment project.

statement of cash flows   The portion of a financial statement that reports only on cash receipts and cash payments; it reveals the relationship of net income, shown on the operating statement, to changes in cash balances.

statement of changes in financial position   A description of changes on a balance sheet from one accounting period to another; a measurement of the resources provided during an accounting period and the uses to which they were put.

statement of retained earnings   This reconciles the balance of retained earnings from the beginning of the year to the end.

straight-line depreciation   A method of depreciation in which an expense is recognized in equal amounts over the useful life of the asset.

straight-line rents   The amounts recorded to amortize rents evenly over the term of a lease.

subordinated bonds or debentures   These are junior to the other creditors in exercising claims against assets.

tangible asssets   Physical items that can be seen and touched, such as property, plant, and equipment; usually called *fixed assets*.

tenant improvement allowances   Provisions in a lease in which the landlord agrees to pay for certain changes to enhance a tenant's space.

10K   The required annual filing of a publicly owned and traded company's financial statement, and all supporting schedules, with the Securities and Exchange Commission (SEC) for public disclosure.

10Q   The required filing by a publicly owned and traded company of a quarterly financial statement with the Securities and Exchange Commission (SEC) for public disclosure.

term   The length of a loan.

time value of money   The concept that the same amount of money is better to have now than at some future date, because now that amount can be invested or used immediately.

transactions   A transfer of value to or from a company, the most basic kinds being sales and purchases.

trial balance   A list of all open accounts in a general ledger, with their balances, used in the preparation of financial statements; when it is complete, debits and credits will prove equal.

triple net lease   A lease in which, unlike a gross lease or a lease with caps, the tenant pays 100 percent of its share of all taxes, insurance, and maintenance associated with a shopping center.

unnatural breakpoint   A set sales hurdle, negotiated and entered in a lease, that can be used to determine payments by a tenant to the landlord unrelated to the tenant's actual breakpoint.

useful life   The period of time that a purchaser expects to get value for a particular purchase, regardless of how long it is actually in use.

vacancy loss   A rate, which an appraiser applies to gross revenue, that recognizes that a property will not always be 100 percent leased; for example, a 5 percent vacancy loss rate anticipates that the shopping center is likely to be 95 percent occupied.

value   A determination about a company, set in the marketplace, that is based on the income it produces year after year; it is calculated by dividing net operating income (NOI) by the cap (capitalization) rate.

working capital   The difference between current assets and current liabilities.

zero-based budgeting   A method of developing a budget without basing it on any previous year's budget; the starting point for each item is zero, and the requirements for the next year's operation must be defined, contracts rebid, and other research performed to come up with the most up-to-date information.